# What Kind of Friendship?

# What Kind of Friendship?

Christian Responses to Tariq Ramadan's
Call for Reform within Islam

Tom Wilson

WIPF & STOCK · Eugene, Oregon

WHAT KIND OF FRIENDSHIP?
Christian Responses to Tariq Ramadan's Call for Reform within Islam

Copyright © 2015 Tom Wilson. All rights reserved. Except for brief quotations in critical publications or reviews, no part of this book may be reproduced in any manner without prior written permission from the publisher. Write: Permissions, Wipf and Stock Publishers, 199 W. 8th Ave., Suite 3, Eugene, OR 97401.

THE HOLY BIBLE, NEW INTERNATIONAL VERSION® NIV.® Copyright © 1973, 1978, 1984 by International Bible Society.® Used by permission. All rights reserved worldwide.

Wipf & Stock
An Imprint of Wipf and Stock Publishers
199 W. 8th Ave., Suite 3
Eugene, OR 97401

www.wipfandstock.com

ISBN 13: 978-1-4982-2444-4

Manufactured in the U.S.A.                                          08/12/2015

This book is dedicated to all those who have taught me more about my own faith and their faith, especially to those Muslims who have taken the time to invest in our friendship and discuss where we agree and where we differ.

# Contents

1  Clearing the Ground | 1
2  The Place of Witness | 18
3  The Four Practical Pillars | 33
4  Steps for Social Engagement | 50
5  Ethics and Medical Science | 65
6  Culture and the Arts | 79
7  Women: Traditions and Liberation | 95
8  Ecology and Economy | 108
9  Society, Education, and Power | 125
10 Ethics and Universals | 139

*Bibliography* | 145

# 1

# Clearing the Ground

WHAT SORT OF RELATIONSHIP should Christians expect to have with Muslims? It is common to talk about how Jews, Christians, and Muslims are all "children of Abraham," in the sense that adherents to all these three great world religions trace a common ancestry to this one figure. But membership of the same family is no guarantee of a good relationship; indeed it can be the reason for a very bad one. Families often do not get along: two brothers I knew got into an inheritance dispute that became so negative they threatened to kill each other. Christians and Muslims may all be "children of Abraham," but we need more than common ancestry to ensure a good relationship. Moreover, the idea of our being allies in a common struggle against secularism has some merit, but would also imply that we might be enemies at some point, as alliances are often fragile and can crumble under pressure.

We do not choose our family, but we can choose our friends. I have chosen the theme of friendship as a metaphor to explore the relationship between Christians and Muslims. I have some very good friends who are Muslim. We disagree about many things, including our understanding of whom Jesus is and what it means to follow him. But we also agree about many things, such as the importance of care for creation, care for our fellow human beings, and work to improve the neighborhood and city we live in. We are friends who work together and disagree without falling out. My friendship with Muslims is the basis for this book.

## What Kind of Friendship?

At the outset of a book that is an exercise in Christian-Muslim conversation it is important to be clear what I am attempting to do, and what I am not attempting to do, in writing. This is not a guide to Islam in general, or to specific groups within Islam. There are many books that do that.[1] This is not an attempt to prove Islam wrong, or to trumpet the superiority of Christianity.

What I am doing is reading the published writings of Tariq Ramadan and reacting to them. In 2004 Tariq Ramadan was hailed by Time magazine as one of the one hundred most influential people in the world. His writing and public lectures on reform within Islam have made him an internationally recognized figure within Islam. He is known as an advocate of reform who is also clear about his own Muslim identity. In this book I am taking his writings as a single discrete corpus of texts that I can read and engage with, in order to formulate a Christian response to calls for reform within Islam, to give one answer to the question "What sort of friendship should Christians have with Muslims?"

I am writing as a convinced and practicing Christian who is an evangelical minister within the Church of England. I have, of course, included the views of other scholars to facilitate a wider and richer conversation, but practicalities have limited the number of perspectives it is possible to engage with. I am not claiming anything definitive in my writing, but rather have engaged in a process of learning and discovery. I am not seeking to prove myself right and Ramadan, or anyone else, wrong. I am seeking to learn and grow in my faith as a Christian through engaging with the thoughts of someone who is both very different and also in some ways quite similar to myself. I have described the book as a "conversation," a term that is in some ways completely misleading, because although I have talked with people in writing this book, my "conversation" with Tariq Ramadan has consisted almost entirely of my reading his published work and then responding to what I think he is saying. Sometimes I have disagreed with him and at other times I have agreed.

I agree with Ramadan, for example, that we can only see the world from our own perspective. We must begin any comparative conversation by admitting that we have nothing more than our own point of view, which shapes our ideas, perceptions, and imagination.[2] I can only see the world from my own perspective, and I can never fully enter into someone else's

---

1. Such as Geaves, *Islam Today* or Bowen, *Medina in Birmingham, Najaf in Brent*.
2. Ramadan, *The Quest for Meaning*, x.

perspective or viewpoint. Tariq Ramadan and I have a different perspective on many things, including the authority of the Qur'an, our understanding of whom Jesus is, and the style of prayer we think it is most appropriate to engage in, either individually or in a gathered congregation. From reading his work, I think we may also share many perspectives and concerns, including a dislike of hypocritical religion that prioritizes form over substance, a dissatisfaction with the consumerist, hedonistic culture of twenty-first century Britain, and a yearning for a deeper personal spirituality amongst those who claim to practice both Christianity and Islam. We are alike and also very different. Ramadan suggests,

> There can be no universal without diversity: the quest for the ultimate commonality would be pointless if we did not recognize the initial differences that explain just why we have to go in search of the universal.[3]

I agree that a search for common ground should begin with a clear, honest recognition of difference. As part of a ground clearing exercise in preparation for deeper engagement, it is important to recognize that there are fundamental points of diversity between Christians and Muslims, areas about which we can never fully agree whilst also remaining faithful to our own traditions. Muslims are clear that Muhammad is the Messenger of God, the last Prophet. Christians are clear that Jesus is the Son of God, the one who died and rose again to atone for our failures. A Christian cannot, in my understanding, remain a Christian whilst simultaneously recognizing Muhammad as the Messenger of God any more than a Muslim can remain fully Muslim whilst recognizing Jesus as the Son of God in the Christian understanding of that title. It is possible to be a secret believer, but at the very least, there must be some kind of faith. In John's Gospel, Joseph of Arimathea and Nicodemus appear to be "secret disciples" who privately follow Jesus, but make no public profession of faith (John 19:38–9). In modern day Somalia, individuals may have a devout faith in Jesus (whom they call *Isa*) but outwardly appear to behave as Muslims. But even when faith is secret, clear decisions have been made about the status of Muhammad and of Jesus. We must begin by recognizing the reality of our diversity of opinion. The differences may be only a few inches wide, but they are miles deep. Recognition of difference does not necessarily lead to combative conflict. It may lead to creative dialogue, to meaningful engagement, to a quest to find what values we share, and what

---

3. Ramadan, *The Quest for Meaning*, 15.

things we can learn from each other. It may lead to friendly recognition of differences while also working together for a common cause.

I often find that those completely outside of the Christian Church present a great challenge to my personal Christian discipleship. To give one simple example, the dedication of Muslims I know personally to prayer and fasting challenges my own spiritual disciplines. Challenged by these people, I am engaging with Ramadan to learn, not to score points.

This is an important difference, one that must be borne in mind throughout this exercise of reading Ramadan as a Christian. As Ramadan puts it:

> When we compare *our* theoretical ideals with *their* weaknesses and *their* inconsistencies, we become involved in a theologico-philosophical competition, and we have already won it: the intention behind the comparison is malicious and its terms are biased.[4]

If we come not for conversation but for combat, then we will find a fight. If we come to prove our own superiority, then we will automatically rig the comparison such that our superiority is bound to become self-evident. But if we come in humility, prepared to compare strength with strength and weakness with weakness, then we come in a position to learn. The illusion of a fair comparison that is in reality biased is far worse than the recognition of a biased comparison that is striving to be fair. Nothing I have read of Ramadan's writing has convinced me to abandon my Christian faith and become a Muslim. But much of what I have read has shown me areas where I need to work hard, in the power of God's Holy Spirit, at living out a more authentic expression of my own Christian faith. I know my reading is biased, but I am striving to be fair in how I read Ramadan, to engage with his strongest arguments, not his weakest. I am trying to avoid scoring cheap points and aiming to challenge myself.

Ramadan discusses the need for establishing common ground, spaces of intersection where we meet on equal terms.[5] This requires curiosity, a desire to truly understand what your conversational protagonist thinks and why they think that. This does not mean abandoning one's own point of view, but it does mean taking the necessary steps to understand other peoples' perspectives. I do not think this is to advocate relativism or a pluralistic understanding of religion, but rather to engage in honest, adult

---

4. Ramadan, *The Quest for Meaning*, 23, emphasis original.
5. Ibid., 24–5.

conversation about difference, in order to understand and to grow personally. This is what I am trying to do as I read Ramadan.

Finally, I am writing with a desire to learn, but also from a particular Christian perspective. Broadly speaking, Christians adopt one of three attitudes to other faiths: exclusivism, which believes salvation only comes through explicitly stated faith in Jesus Christ; inclusivism, which believes salvation only comes through Jesus, but one does not have to make an explicit, public profession of faith in order to be saved by him; and pluralism, which believes salvation can come in many different ways.

## CHRISTIAN VIEWS OF OTHER RELIGIONS

I find arguments for pluralism unconvincing, sharing Gavin D'Costa's reservations that pluralism often fails to hold to its own standards and goals of being welcoming and inclusive. That is to say that espoused pluralism can often become an epistemologically exclusive position that dismisses other viewpoints, which might be regarded as an arrogant fashion, and furthermore fails to remain within the bounds of Christian orthodoxy.[6] I am also unconvinced by the story of the blind men and the elephant, which is often used to defend a pluralist standpoint. The story goes that different blind men are all touching an elephant and describe it from their very limited perspectives. So the one who is touching the trunk describes a very different elephant from the one who is touching the tail, or a leg, or a tusk. In the story, the elephant is God and the religions of the world are the blind men. But as Newbigin explains, the story is told from the point of view of those watching the blind men.[7] The watchers are not blind but can see that the blind men are unable to grasp the full reality of the elephant and are only able to get hold of part of the truth. The story is told from the perspective of one who claims to see more than all the religions of the world and so makes an incredibly arrogant claim to see the full truth that all the world's religions are only groping after. Although not all pluralists are arrogant, they must all recognize that their faith position of many paths to God is epistemologically as exclusive as any other view.

Similarly, I am uncertain about Karl Rahner's notion of anonymous Christians, especially the idea of Christians including non-Christians entirely on Christian grounds. I concur with Greggs that Christians should not

---

6. D'Costa, *Christianity and World Religions*, 9–18.
7. Newbigin, *The Gospel in a Pluralist Society,* 9–10.

offer dictates or advice to other religions, as to do so would be to include by "doing violence to the otherness of the other."[8] My concern about inclusivism is that, although it appears to be superficially welcoming, it is actually arrogant, because it dismisses the sincere attempts of people to attain salvation by following a particular religious path (be it Muslim, Hindu, Buddhist, or whatever else) and instead says that those efforts are irrelevant, because salvation comes through Christ. An inclusivist may not intend to belittle other faiths, but I think they are in grave danger of doing so.

I am exclusivist, and my understanding of a Christian response to other religions is strongly influenced by Lesslie Newbigin. He argues that we must hold the two truths of God's grace and human sin in tension. Furthermore, he suggests it is not our place to ask what happens when a non-Christian dies, as that is God's decision. Newbigin finds the question itself reductionist, arguing that it reduces a person to a soul that needs an eternal destination, and overly focused on human beings instead of on God and his glory. These are concerns I share.

Newbigin suggests four things a Christian should look for in contact with those who are not Christians.[9] First, we should expect, look for, and welcome signs of the grace of God in their lives. Second, we should cooperate with everyone, regardless of faith position, on projects that are in accordance with a Christian view of God's purpose in history. Third, this cooperation provides the context for real dialogue, which is the aim of this book. Fourth, we bring the story of Jesus, and of the Bible, told on request and in response to a concrete, real-life situation. He summarizes the nature of this position as follows:

> The position which I have outlined is exclusivist in the sense that it affirms the unique truth of the revelation in Jesus Christ, but it is not exclusivist in the sense of denying the possibility of the salvation of the non-Christian. It is inclusivist in the sense that it refuses to limit the saving grace of God to members of the Christian church, but it rejects the inclusivism which regards the non-Christian religions as vehicles of salvation. It is pluralist in the sense of acknowledging the gracious work of God in the lives of all human beings, but it rejects a pluralism which denies the uniqueness and decisiveness of what God has done in Jesus Christ.

---

8. Greggs, "The Lord of All," 45–6.
9. Newbigin, *The Gospel in a Pluralist Society*, 180–3.

I endeavor to engage with those of other faiths with what Daniel Strange terms "bold humility," a stance that begins by seeking understanding of other religions through a biblical world view, before applying the unique truths of the gospel of Jesus Christ to those religions in order to bring salvation to them. I recognize that plurality is not something to fear or shy away from, but rather to be celebrated, investigated, and understood as a blessing from God "whose very being is characterized by diversity in unity and unity in diversity."[10]

Amos Yong correctly observes that, "Most theologians are far too complex to fit neatly into exclusivist, inclusivist or pluralist camps,"[11] a position I concur with and echoes the quote from Newbigin above. When encountering the other, I seek both to learn from them and to bring that learning into an encounter with the Christian faith, and these twin aims are at the heart of this book.

## AIMS OF THE BOOK

The remainder of this chapter continues the ground clearing exercise by discussing the complex political culture in which it has been written before tackling two common concerns about Islam, namely the issues of *shariah* law and of *jihad*, and giving a brief reflection on honor and shame. The rest of the text is divided into two parts. The first three chapters deal with preliminary issues, concentrating on the core Islamic religious beliefs and discussing steps for social engagement. The second part contains six chapters, each of which engages with a separate chapter in a book by Tariq Ramadan entitled *Radical Reform*. They concern issues where Ramadan believes there is a need for reform amongst the Muslim world and cover medical ethics, culture and the arts, the role of women in society, ecology and the economy, society, education and power, and finally ethics and universals. This closing chapter draws together the threads of the previous discussion, outlining a vision for how Christians and Muslims can engage together in transforming our world for the better.

In each chapter I outline Ramadan's own views, commenting both on my personal response to them and also engaging with representative Christian scholars, primarily from the Protestant tradition. I am well aware that Ramadan is not a definitive Islamic spokesperson for many of the issues

---

10. Strange, *For Their Rock is not as Our Rock*, 26.
11. Yong, *Hospitality and the Other*, 66.

he covers, and indeed at times he covers topics about which neither he or I have any technical knowledge or expertise. I am not claiming to provide the last word on any of the topics above, but rather to provide prompts to encourage open conversation. I have chosen to write this book because I read a lot of Tariq Ramadan's work when writing my PhD.[12] In some ways he is a representative orthodox, practicing Muslim. But in others he is quite unusual, for the British context at least. He is creative and open in how he engages with certain issues, far more so than the largely conservative Muslim majority in the UK.

## THE COMPLEX POLITICAL CLIMATE

Any book that comments in detail about specific situations within the complex political climate that faces Islam today is likely to be out of date by the time it is actually published. As I write, the so-called *Islamic State* in Iraq is the particular focus of Western media attention, but not so long ago, it was *Boko Haram* in Nigeria, attacks on the offices of the French satirical magazine *Charlie Hebdo* in Paris, a hostage incident in a café in Sydney, and before that the war in Syria, the war Afghanistan, the situation in Iran, and so on. Events move quickly and the factors that influence them are many and complex. This is not a book on geo-politics, and I am not especially qualified to comment on these situations. My observations are more about the global nature of the situation. Actions in Pakistan, Syria, Nigeria, Iraq, Afghanistan, to name but a few countries, all have a direct impact on the community I live and work amongst. Direct because people have links with family and friends in those countries. Direct because they themselves may recently have been there, may plan to go there, or may have just escaped from there. We live in a very connected world and when Christians speak about Muslims in general, they must be aware that they may be speaking about the family and friends of their own neighbors.

To some extent, the issues facing Muslims in the West are those faced by any group of migrants. Thus Doug Saunders argues for the *Myth of the Muslim Tide*, suggesting that Muslims are simply the latest in a long line of migrants to Western countries, all of whom have initially faced prejudice on arrival, but have later been accepted and become part of the normal fabric of society. There is much truth in his argument. If my parents' parents were born in the UK, then rather than describe me as a "third generation

---

12. Wilson, *Hospitality and Translation*.

migrant" it would be more accurate to describe me simply as British, albeit with a migrant heritage. Most Brits have a migrant heritage, albeit of many generations. Those whose migrant heritage is more ancient are perhaps suspicious of those whose family has only lived in the country for a few generations, but that does not mean they are not citizens of the country. The complexity of personal and group identity must be recognized and acknowledged.

Cesari argues that Muslims are seen as both internal and external enemies of the West.[13] Internal because they fail to integrate, and Islam is held to be incompatible with Western values of freedom and equality and with Western culture. External because they are responsible for international terrorism and they have external allegiances to the Muslim *ummah* that makes them a threat to national security. Although I regard such suggestions as an oversimplification of reality, many people do hold these views, and Tariq Ramadan's work is an attempt to counter them. He argues that binary views of the world, of West versus East (however they are defined) are inaccurate caricatures. He adds that what is especially noticeable is how what he calls the "Arab Awakening" redefined this binary categorization: those who wanted revolution were suddenly viewed as somehow Western because they aspired to more democratic rule. He wryly adds:

> As pendulum swings go, it was spectacular: only yesterday Muslims were the alterity against which the West defined itself; now they had become the *alter ego* of the Western Universal, allowing the West to celebrate itself.[14]

But even though the pendulum had swung, Ramadan argues that it remained on the same binary axis; it was simply that Muslims had now become part of "us" rather than part of the "other." Now that the Arab Spring has not produced what perhaps some hoped for, perhaps the pendulum has swung back to complete other?

What should Christians make of this fraught political situation? First, we must get our facts right. Christianity is not a Western religion. People who live in Western countries may be Christian, but the overwhelming majority of Christians do not live in the West, and Christianity itself originated in the region now termed the Middle East. The work of scholar Kenneth Bailey provides a great introduction to this fact. Second, although I have

---

13. Cesari, *Why the West Fears Islam*, 1–20.
14. Ramadan, *The Arab Awakening*, 16.

used the labels "East" and "West" in the discussion so far, we must recognize how problematic they are. East and West are directions that indicate a perspective, a decision as to where the center lies. Perhaps they are becoming more problematic than helpful for discussing complex geo-political realities. Where shorthand phrases are accurate labels, they are useful, but where they caricature beyond reality, they are much less so.

Third, we must acknowledge the suffering many people face in many situations. Whilst many of my Muslim acquaintances argue that Islam is a religion of peace, it is undoubtedly the case that Christians are particular targets for organizations like *Boko Haram*. Christianity is in danger of being wiped out in countries such as Iraq and Syria, countries which have a much richer Christian heritage than the UK. We should offer financial assistance, pray, and campaign on their behalf, maybe even go ourselves if it is appropriate and we can find a suitable agency to support us. Moreover, we should challenge the bias of our media. Between the 7th and 9th of January 2015, sixteen people were killed and twenty-three were injured in Paris in incidents related to Islamist terrorism. Around the same time, *Boko Haram* in Nigeria killed approximately two thousand people in the town of Baga, near the border with Chad. Millions marched in Paris in support of the freedom of the Press, but no such demonstrations were forthcoming in Nigeria. As Christians we believe that every human being is made in the image of God, but do we challenge our news media when they focus only on those like us?

Fourth, we have to have the difficult conversations. Many British Muslims argue Islam is entirely a religion of peace. They suggest that what is happening throughout the world has nothing to do with Islam. They do have something of a point. Religion can be used as an overly simplistic label in order to create a false binary division and rally people to a particular cause. In the case of Christianity, it is commonly recognized that the decades long conflict in Northern Ireland is not simply about how the Christian faith should be understood or practiced. In 1985, an Acholi woman in northern Uganda, Alice Auma, claimed possession by a Christian spirit called Lakwena. She was a local Christian healer, who became the driving force behind the Holy Spirit Movement, from which the Lord's Resistance Army, which still operates in northern Uganda and the surrounding region, sprang.[15] Initially the Holy Spirit Movement claimed divine protection and utilized Christianity imagery, but few would say either the Holy Spirit

---

15. Behrend, *Alice Lakwena and the Holy Spirits*.

Movement or its successor, the Lord's Resistance Army are recognizably Christian. Equally, the anti-Balaka movement in the Central African Republic is sometimes described as Christian (because of their opposition to the Seleka movement, many of whom are Muslim), but using religious labels for either group is over-simplistic. Similar points could be made about the civil war in Syria and other conflicts. Whilst I accept this caveat, the challenging conversation about Islam remains. Violence is being done in the name of the religion, and unless articulate, erudite, convincing Muslims present an alternative narrative, which is rooted in the Qur'an and the *Sunnah*, doubts about assertions that Islam is a religion of peace will remain. As Christians we must educate ourselves as to the differences within Islam. Invariably, those who do violence in the name of Islam are *salafist* or *Wahabi* in their theology. These are literalist, conservative, reformist groups within Islam who aim to exactly replicate life in seventh century Arabic in the twenty-first century world. Perhaps naming the particular subgroup as a distinct force will help nuance our understanding and not tar all Muslims with a brush that is irrelevant to them. But even then, we must recognize not all *salafists* are necessarily advocates of violence.

The history of how Islam initially spread is a case in point of what to say about Islam and peace. Having established himself securely in Medina, having won a number of battles and demonstrated his military capabilities, Muhammad then chose to return to Mecca. Tariq Ramadan recounts how this took place

> Muhammad had segmented his army into divisions that encircles the city and closed in on the center together. A few Quraysh groups posted themselves on the hills, led by Suhayl, Ikrimah, and Safwan, but after the first confrontations, they realized that resisting was pointless. . . . The Prophet had demanded that no fighting or battle should take place on that day, which he called 'the day of mercy.'[16]

Muhammad entered Mecca at the head of his military forces, removed all the idols from the *Kaba'a*, and established his rule. Ramadan is keen to point out the lack of violence, the fact that Muhammad prayed on his return to Mecca, and the peaceful transition of power. But it was nevertheless a transition of power that was backed up by the threat of military force. The army may not have killed anyone, but they were still present. As Islam spread during the next few decades it was as much by violence as by any

16. Ramadan, *In the Footsteps of the Prophet*, 177.

## What Kind of Friendship?

other means. Initially, Christianity spread by subverting the power of the Roman Empire, although centuries later it was itself arguably subverted by the power of Rome. By contrast, Islam's roots lie in a top-down power grab, which is perhaps a motivating factor for many *salafist* groups today.

Christians must have the courage to speak the truth, with gentleness and respect, in a spirit of love and compassion. We are slowly coming to recognize the logs in our own eyes, the love of power and status and personal wealth that have little to do with the Gospel of Jesus Christ. We cannot reform Islam, and should not try to. But we can encourage those who seek to do so, and reform cannot happen without the truth of history and of the present situation being acknowledged. Christians must work hard at being authentic disciples of Jesus and challenging violent oppression in all its forms.

## WHAT DO MUSLIMS MEAN BY JIHAD?

The Arabic word *jihad* means "struggle" or "resistance." For Ramadan, it is partly a personal exercise, mastering the self, one's ego, and violence. It also has a social dimension, struggling for justice and working against discrimination and unemployment. Third, he argues *jihad* has a political aspect, defending civil responsibilities, promoting pluralism, and freedom of expression and democracy. Fourth, the economic *jihad*, "action against speculation, monopolies and neocolonialism." Fifth, cultural: promoting the arts, in so far as they respect dignity of conscience and human values.[17] *Jihad*, in this view, has nothing to do with violence. It is, essentially, the *radical reform* that will be discussed at some length in this book. Elsewhere, Ramadan calls for intellectual *jihad* as part of the Arab Awakening, a serious intellectual effort to re-envision the place of Islam within Muslim majority societies, bringing about "a multidimensional culture of dignity and peace" which is free both from Western neocolonialism and also despotic local rulers.[18]

It is difficult to argue against these definitions of *jihad*. Indeed, there are related struggles that Christians may themselves wish to engage in: the purification of the self, personal transformation into a greater likeness of Jesus Christ, whilst at the same time working in the power of the Spirit to realize the fullness of the Kingdom of God in the social, political,

---

17. Ramadan, *Western Muslims and the Future of Islam*, 113.
18. Ramadan, *The Arab Awakening*, 148.

economic, and cultural world. Flannagan argues that Christians should work hard to bring the Kingdom of God in all its fullness into seven interrelated spheres: government, media, arts, education, family, religion, and business.[19] Christians recognize that change does not come easily; it can be a real struggle to be a faithful follower of Jesus and to bring about transformation in his name. Flannagan's is a very similar message to that which Ramadan advocates. But not all Muslims understand *jihad* entirely in this way. The question remains, what about other understandings of *jihad*?

Ramadan recognizes the diversity within Islam. There are different interpretations of Islam, including traditionalist, literalist, reformist, rationalist, political, and Sufi, which are not mutually exclusive, but rather reinforcing. Islam is present in a wide variety of nations and cultures, and so has many different local expressions. Ramadan envisions "a single, fundamental religious reference expressed diversely through different historical periods, intellectual perspectives and cultures."[20] For some who call themselves Muslims, *jihad* means war against non-Muslims, and indeed some Muslims who are not deemed sufficiently pious. How could Islam respond to this? There are, perhaps, two options. First, to accept theirs is also a valid interpretation of Islam or second, to explicitly condemn and refute their interpretation through reference to sacred texts and lived example. A Muslim may hold either view and try to ignore this understanding of *jihad*, but silence can be misinterpreted as acceptance when it does not actually indicate this. Speaking out is the only way to remove the ambiguity.

Ramadan does speak out. His website includes a number of videos where clear statements of his view of *jihad* are expressed. He has analyzed at some length the causes of Islamism.[21] Not everyone will agree with all the detail of his argument, but the broad picture is accurate. His strategy appears to be to explain the phenomena and to offer an alternative vision. I am left wondering whether a clear Qur'anic rebuttal is also needed. Perhaps, as with Ramadan's call for the moratorium on *hudud* (the Islamic penal code, discussed below) rather than an outright ban, this is more than he feels able to offer. But without such an argument, it is difficult to see how a clear case can be made that violent *jihad* has no place in Islam.

Christians will not help this situation if they simply condemn from a distance. Undoubtedly, Christians need to engage in serious study of

19. Flannagan, *Those Who Show Up*, 89.
20. Ramadan, *The Arab Awakening*, 74.
21. Ibid., 72–105.

Qur'anic texts themselves, in order to be better able to respond to the issues. Moreover, Christians should build strong relationships with Muslims, relationships where difficult questions can be honestly and openly discussed. Christians have a range of views on the place of war, and it would be foolish to pretend otherwise. History (let alone the present) is not entirely on our side if we condemn violence in the name of religion as though it were an exclusively *salafi* Islamist phenomenon. Our response to the issue of *jihad* must, at the very least, include articulating a clear Christian vision of how society can be organized without recourse to violence, challenging and encouraging our Muslim friends and neighbors as to whether they can do the same from their perspective and defending those who are defenseless, wherever and whoever they may be. This book is written in the hope of equipping some to begin the work of building the necessary relationships from which an alternative vision can emerge.

## WHAT ABOUT SHARIA LAW?

In 2008, the then Archbishop of Canterbury was misquoted and misunderstood by sections of the British media (hardly an uncommon experience for an Archbishop). It was reported that he had suggested Britain should adopt *sharia* law, when he had done no such thing. Instead he had simply recognized that there should be space for the expression of religious conscience within the exercise of the law. *Sharia* law is a very emotive issue in the UK, as for most people, *sharia* law is equated almost exclusively with harsh punishments for certain crimes, notably stoning for adultery, or cutting the hand off a thief. In fact, as Ramadan notes, *sharia*, is better understood as:

> The expression of individual and collective faithfulness, in time, for those who are trying in awareness to draw near to the ideal of the Source that is God.... *Shariah* is not only the expression of the universal principles of Islam but the framework and the thinking that makes for their actualization in human history.[22]

One common translation of *sharia* is "the Way." It is less an established complete code (although it does include prescriptions related to certain actions), and more guidance for how to live a genuinely Islamic way of life. There are certain areas within *sharia* which most British people, Muslim

---

22. Ramadan, *Western Muslims and the Future of Islam*, 32.

or otherwise, would find reprehensible, and I will return to the issue of the Islamic penal code at a later stage.

It is important that Christians recognize that, whilst we may have certain prejudices about Muslims, it is just as likely that Muslims have as many about Christians, and they may be equally misinformed. A Muslim might think that most people in the UK are practicing Christians who have no problem with drunkenness, sexually promiscuous behavior, or that they wholeheartedly endorse violence against Muslims in countries such as Iraq simply because those are Muslim nations. Misunderstandings can only be clarified in genuine, honest dialogue and real, courageous relationships.

## HONOR AND SHAME

Any Christian engaging with Muslims would benefit from at least a notional understanding of the issues of honor and shame. These are complex topics, best learnt about through lived experience, but a few brief orientating comments may be of some assistance.

Honor is public esteem, and shame the removal of that esteem. All societies operate with some form of honor and shame, but those in the Mediterranean world operate in a distinctive way. Throughout the Mediterranean world in particular, male honor is primarily derived from the struggle to maintain intact the honor of kinswomen, which means male reputation depends primarily on the sexual conduct of female family members. Economic success, physical prowess, family autonomy, as well as characteristics such as hospitality, integrity, and generosity all contribute to the ascription of honor, but in a more secondary fashion. There is, of course, some variation in exactly how this manifests itself, but the central premise remains constant.

As Pattison notes, the capacity to feel shame is integral to being human, marking the boundaries of self with others and community.[23] Developing a sense of shame is the means by which we internalize the expectations of our family and society. Taking the example of female sexual purity discussed thus far, in societies where the honor/shame paradigm operates, expectations regarding both male and female behavior are internalized from a young age and define all social interaction between the two genders. Shame is a complex, multifaceted phenomenon. It begins with the body and the self, but is also influenced by wider social, political, and cultural causes

---

23. Pattison, *Saving Face*, 58.

and effects.[24] Some individuals feel a strong sense of shame whenever they transgress boundaries set by either themselves or their society.

Shame must be distinguished from guilt. Tangney and Dearing suggest differentiating between guilt about specific behaviors in contrast with shame about the self.[25] They argue that the role of the self is central in understanding the difference between shame and guilt. Shame involves fairly global negative evaluations of the self, but guilt involves a more articulated condemnation of a specific behavior. They over-simplify for clarity, proposing that shame concerns "who I am" while guilt relates to "what I did."[26] Shame is therefore not simply about public exposure, but also about personal evaluation. Thus those reporting experiences of shame tended to focus on others' evaluation of the self, while guilt concerned more one's effect on others.

It is an oversimplification of reality to discuss groups of individuals (such as Muslims) as all displaying the same behavior. Moreover, it is inaccurate to describe people in terms of a singular affiliation; I am a Christian and a man, but there is more to my identity than these two facets of it. We are all complex individuals with multiple aspects to our identity. Nevertheless, it is generally true that many societies in which Islam is the dominant religion operate more in terms of shame than of guilt. This has a big impact on behavior, especially in the concept of how an individual's behavior directly affects the status of the groups to which he belongs.[27] Thus for an individual to engage in shameful behavior impacts not only himself, but also his extended family and potentially his whole people group.[28]

Christians who wish to engage with Muslims in discussing the topics raised by this book would benefit from awareness of the dynamics of honor and shame. Not every issue can be discussed in a public meeting; far more profitable conversations may be had in a more personal setting. Conversations with individual Muslim friends have given me a much clearer understanding of the issues related to drug taking in the Muslim community I live amongst than any formal conversations with an imam during a public mosque visit I have organized.

---

24. Ibid., 61.
25. Tangney and Dearing, *Shame and Guilt*, 8.
26. Ibid., 24.
27. Muller, *Honor and Shame*, 46–55.
28. Musk, *Touching the Soul of Islam*, 67–88.

### Clearing the Ground
## WHAT KIND OF FRIENDSHIP?

At the conclusion of each chapter, I will return to my title question, and ask what kind of friendship has the chapter envisioned. This first chapter suggests that friendship between Christians and Muslims must be based on a willingness to ask hard questions, to challenge each other, but also to understand each other, especially to recognize the importance of cultural influences on behavior. We must be prepared to take risks, to acknowledge differences, but still remain friends.

# 2

# The Place of Witness

Is it possible, or even desirable, for Muslims to be part of Western society? In one sense this question makes little or no sense. Take Britain as an example. Millions of Muslims are British citizens; whilst their parents or grandparents or great grandparents were born in another country, they were born in the UK and so are British citizens, and therefore by definition are a part of British society. They speak with a British accent, support British sporting teams, enjoy British television and speak only English. The statistical evidence is difficult to deny, but it is also true that some groups of Muslims, whilst they may be British born, spend relatively little time interacting beyond their own defined social circle. One of my Muslim friends in Gloucester is quite conservative in his theology, and despite the presence of many *halal* butchers close to where we both live, he travels eighty-five miles to Leicester to buy meat from a butcher whom he trusts. He works in a further education college, but outside of this part time job, inhabits a narrowly defined social sphere. There are doubtless many other individuals whose religious (or other) views mean many of their daily interactions are within a very defined space. Whilst most of us live within a relatively small social sphere, how exactly should we engage with the wider world?

In this opening section, I will engage with Tariq Ramadan's argument that Muslims have a duty to regard Western society as a place of witness, or "abode of testimony," as he describes it. The argument is put forward in greatest detail in *Western Muslims and the Future of Islam*, and I will mainly discuss the argument as it is developed there. I first describe Ramadan's critique of Muslim thinking about how to engage with the West, second, I set out his vision before, lastly, offering my own responses to that vision.

Ramadan's understanding of Islam is of faithfulness rather than literalist imitation. Using the analogy of translation, I suggest he is against a word for word approach, and in favor of a more dynamic stance on translating faith into everyday life. He suggests that human beings, through their own reason and critical engagement with the sources of Islamic teaching can put forward original proposals for how to live as authentic Muslims who are also in tune with their own context.

There are a number of sources Muslims refer to. The first is the Qur'an. The second is the *Sunnah* (the way of life expected of a Muslim). The third source of Islamic teaching is commentary on the first two. Muslims must work hard at this process of understanding. Ramadan argues they should avoid a defensive approach, steering clear of "an integration that depends on a collection of legal opinions aimed at protection," and instead endeavor to follow a route that allows Muslims to establish themselves freely and confidently and that opens the way for them to make a contribution to wider society.[1] This can be clearly seen in his discussion of how Muslims should imitate the Prophet's style of dress. Those who favor a more literalist stance argue that a faithful Muslim should dress exactly as the Prophet did, including wearing a silver signet ring and dying their hair and beard orange with henna (needless to say, there is an implicit sexist assumption here that only a man can be a true disciple of the Prophet). Ramadan's more dynamic approach suggests that the Prophet's injunction concerning modest dress can be interpreted to include any clothing that is appropriate for the society in which one lives.[2]

This dynamic approach is also evident in his expectations regarding societal interaction. The traditional Muslim approach to relations between and within societies was to divide the world into two opposing spheres: the *dar al-islam* and the *dar al-harb*, normally translated as the "house of Islam" and the "house of war." Ramadan suggests that the concepts are not found in the Qur'an or in the *Sunnah*, but that they were developed by the *ulama*, scholars who specialized in Islamic sciences, in response to the geo-political realities of the expanding Islamic empire.[3] When Islam was a

---

1. Ramadan, *Western Muslims and the Future of Islam*, 62.
2. Ramadan, *Radical Reform*, 20.
3. Ramadan, *Western Muslims and the Future of Islam*, 63.

## What Kind of Friendship?

powerful politico-military force, the "house of Islam" opposed "the house of war" by all means, including violence, in order to defend strategic interests for territory, trade, and so forth. Ramadan's point is that these ideas, whilst ancient, are not integral to Islam (although an endnote qualifies his argument, stating the concept of *dar al-harb* is found three times, in two *hadith* (of questionable authenticity). This allows him to conclude that the idea of *dar al-islam* and *dar al-harb* are venerable but not essential to Islam. But what exactly do the terms mean?

Ramadan discusses the criteria necessary to establish a place as *dar al-islam*, suggesting four criteria are relevant for recognizing somewhere to be within the "house of Islam": the population in the country; ownership of the land; the nature of the government; and the laws applied. He notes further that Islamic legal opinion varies as to exactly what is classed as *dar al-islam*, but quotes suggestions including defining *dar al-islam* as "the property of Muslims where the Islamic legal system is applied (even if non-Muslims are in power)" and an understanding that it can include any state where "practicing Muslims are in a position of safety." There are also differences within Islamic thought regarding recognizing a country *dar al-harb*, but there is consensus that where the legal system and government are non-Islamic, that is *dar al-harb*. This means that the population may be majority Muslim, but it may not be *dar al-islam*. Finally, he notes that although the country may be classified as belonging to the "house of war," that does not necessarily mean an actual conflict is taking place.[4]

The classification of a country as being within either *dar al-islam* or *dar al-harb* is therefore not as straightforward as it might first be imagined. These definitional criteria mean that if conditions of safety and security are applied as the primary criteria, then many western countries are more likely to be classified as *dar al-islam* than many "Muslim" countries where there may not be the same freedom of religion. For Ramadan, this exposes a fundamental weakness in the classificatory system, which is predicated on an entirely different world order. Many other Muslims would agree with this, suggesting that there are no truly Muslim countries in the world today, and so there cannot be any countries that are regarded as *dar al-harb*.

In response to these difficulties, some scholars propose the existence of a third area, of *dar al-ahd*, the "abode of treaty." It assumes that there are countries which although they are not Muslim, they have signed a treaty of peace and collaboration with one or more Muslim nations. The existence

---

4. Ramadan, *Western Muslims*, 63–8.

of organizations such as the United Nations or the Organization of African Unity support the case for recognizing the place of *dar al-ahd*.

Ramadan has difficulties with this concept, arguing that the idea of *dar al-ahd* is founded on the existence of *dar al-islam* and *dar al-harb*, for the treaty of peace only exists to prevent a war. He also points out that the same term is used both of treaties between countries and of relations between Muslims and a State, which means the term becomes confused in its precise definition. Third, and most problematic, the idea of a treaty between a Muslim and a non-Muslim State implies that the Muslim is not in his own country. This will in fact perpetuate, rather than solve the problem. A Muslim born in the UK to parents also born in the UK is thus denied his British citizenship, and so the attempt to solve the problem in fact exacerbates it. This leads Ramadan to the conclusion that none of these classifications work, and so he suggests we need a new name for a new world order. He argues:

> We are living in an age of diversity, blending, and extremely deep complexity that cannot be understood or evaluated through a binary prism, which is as much simplistic as reductionist.[5]

Many scholars would agree with this point, and the work of the economist Amartya Sen is but one example. In *Identity and Violence*, Sen critiques the simplistic understanding of the world where people are defined merely by one distinguishing feature, such as religion. We all have complex identities, influenced by multiple factors, of which religion may be one, but ethnicity, geographical location, social class, educational achievement, aspirations, sexual orientation, and employment status are but several more in the melting pot of personal and group identity. A binary prism is a distorted lens through which to view the world. All of us need a much more sophisticated approach. Ramadan himself quotes another example from Sen that illustrates the complexity of identity.[6] Suppose you are a poet and a vegetarian. If you are a dinner guest, then you do not insist on your identity as a poet, and likewise when you attend a poetry circle, you do not introduce yourself as a vegetarian. Your context and situation determine which aspect of your identity you emphasize: requesting a vegetarian meal does not make one more (or less) of a poet; it simply indicates a preference regarding food.

---

5. Ibid., 68.
6. Ramadan, *The Quest for Meaning*, 37.

## What Kind of Friendship?

Ramadan argues that the teachings of Islam are universal, and the previous classificatory systems are all human constructs, which were useful for their own time, but are no longer relevant.[7] So he suggests Muslims must go back to the Qur'an and the *Sunnah*, to the records of the teachings of the Prophet Mohammad, and see if a new understanding can be developed. In developing a contextually relevant understanding of the world, he proposes that the two questions that must be asked are "who are we?" and "what does our religion expect of us as Muslims?"

In developing his understanding of how to respond, Ramadan suggests that any society which guarantees freedom of conscience and worship to Muslims, that protects their physical integrity and their freedom to act in accordance with their convictions, is not in fact a hostile society. He argues that this is true of Europe, where five fundamental rights are guaranteed that allow Muslims to feel at home in their countries of residence: namely "the right to practice Islam, the right to knowledge, the right to establish organizations, the right to autonomous representation, and the right to appeal to law."[8] Speaking in constitutional and legal terms, European society is not anti-Islamic. Of course, that is not to say it is necessarily easy to be a Muslim in the West. First, there is the issue of how to maintain spirituality in a society that is secularized and industrialized, which excludes religion from the public sphere. Second, there is the problem of the public perception and portrayal of Islam as a result of national and international news. Muslims face suspicion and harassment in the West, and these difficulties should not be minimized. The twin challenges of being religious in a secular society and being Muslim in a society that is uneasy with Muslims must not be underestimated.

In Ramadan's view, there have, broadly speaking, been three responses from the *ulama* to the challenge of living in Western European society: first, the old concepts of *dar al-islam* and *dar al-harb* are still valid, even if not every relevant condition has been met. Second, there are those who turn to the concept of *dar al-ahd* (abode of treaty) or *dar al-amn* (abode of safety). Third, there are those who develop the idea of *dar al-dawa*, the abode of invitation to God. Ramadan supports this third idea, but is unconvinced by the name. He suggests Muslims have a duty both to live out their faith and also to engage with the society that is around them, arguing that:

---

7. Ramadan, *Western Muslims*, 69–72.
8. Ibid., 71.

## The Place of Witness

> Wherever a Muslim who declares, 'I bear witness that there is no god but God and Muhammad is His messenger' lives in security and can fulfill his fundamental religious obligations, he is at home, for the Prophet taught us that the world is a mosque.[9]

This leads Ramadan to conclude that Muslims living in the West, both as individuals and as communities gathered together from a diverse range of countries, are not only free to live, but also bear the weight of responsibility to give testimony to their society, based on their faith, as to how to live as a human being created by Allah. Ramadan is uncertain about the concept of *dawa*, because it "has many shades of meaning and is difficult to translate." (He suggests in an endnote that the fundamental concept is of presentation of the message of Islam, but recognizes there are many shades of meaning to the term). Ramadan prefers the notion of *shahada*, testimony, for two reasons: first, one is required to pronounce the *shahada* before two witnesses in order to become a Muslim, and second, because of the Qur'anic injunction to bear witness to the faith before humanity (2:143).

Having settled on his preferred term, *dar al-shahada*, Ramadan then develops six points that support this understanding.[10] First, "In pronouncing the *shahada*, Muslims testify to their faith and state a clear foundation for their identity." It is a summary of a world-view, belief system, and intention for how to live. Second, it is not just the first of the five pillars of Islam; it is the foundation, the rock, on which the other four pillars stand. Third, this means Muslims should be able to respect and comply with the commandments and regulations of their religion, and the observance of what is legitimate and illegitimate in their faith. Fourth,

> To pronounce the *shahada* is to act before God in respect of His creation, for *al-iman* (faith) is in fact a pledge (*amana*). The *shahada* is, in effect, a promise to act in certain way, and to be a person whose word can be trusted and adhered to.

Fifth, Muslims bear witness to the meaning of the *shahada* to their fellow human beings; they should present Islam, the teachings of their faith, as witnesses (*shuhada*), which would include the idea of *dawa*. Sixth, this witness is not simply verbal but includes action. "To bear the *shahada* means to be engaged in society in every area where a need makes itself felt: unemployment, marginalization, delinquency, and so on."

---

9. Ramadan, *Western Muslims*, 72–3.
10. Ibid., 74–5.

This, then, is why Ramadan is so in favor of the concept: it clearly establishes both Muslim identity and Muslim social responsibility in relation to wider society. On a technical note, he suggests that *dar* should not be translated in the limited sense of "a house" or "a dwelling," but rather in the more geographically broad sense of "space," with a sense both of an environment and also of being open to the wider world. A house is, by definition, discrete, closed, and limited, and what is needed is something much more open and free. Muslims should thus regard the area in which they live as a "space of testimony," or as I have termed it "a place of witness," which necessarily means they will be both distinctively Muslim but also actively engaged with the society in which they live. Finally, it is important to note that Ramadan understands Westernization and globalization more in terms of center and periphery than in the sense of two opposing houses, and hence Muslims are called to be witnesses to Islam in both the center and periphery of the world.

Ramadan's conclusion to his discussion sets out his vision clearly:

> For Muslims at the heart of the West, there can be no question of falling back into the old binary vision and looking for enemies; it is rather a matter of finding committed partners like themselves who will make a selection from what Western culture produces in order to promote its positive contributions and resist its destructive by-products at both the human and the ecological level. More generally, it is also a matter of working for the promotion of a true religious and cultural pluralism on an international scale. Many European and American intellectuals are fighting to ensure that the right of civilizations and cultures to exist is in fact respected. Before God, and with all men, in the West Muslims must be with them, *witnesses* engaged in this resistance, for justice, for all human beings, of whatever race, origin, or religion.[11]

Ramadan's fundamental call, therefore, is for Muslims to be witnesses in the society they find themselves. He describes Europe as "an area of responsibility" for Muslims. He concludes that Muslims can no longer hide away or concentrate on protecting themselves or isolating themselves from the world. Instead they must give of themselves to better the societies of which they are part, both as individuals and as a collective group. This sounds very positive, but what would it look like in reality?

---

11. Ibid., 76.

## The Place of Witness

In his account of the life of the Prophet, Ramadan sets out a clear example of the practice of living in *dar al-shahada*, namely the first *hijrah* (journey) from Mecca.[12] In the first years of Islam, while Muhammad and his followers were still resident in Mecca, they experienced a significant degree of persecution from the Quraysh leaders in Mecca, who disliked Muhammad's message of allegiance to one God, as it challenged their belief in many gods, and the status of Mecca as a place people came to in order to worship these gods and receive their blessing. His uncle, Abu Talib, protected Muhammad himself, but many of his followers did not enjoy this luxury. Muhammad therefore suggested that they leave Mecca, and travel to Abyssinia, to seek the protection of the Negus, the Christian king of Abyssinia, who had a reputation for respectful and fair treatment of his people.

Ramadan reports that around one hundred people left Mecca in 615 CE, five years after Muhammad's first revelation, and travelled to Abyssinia. The Quraysh leaders learnt of this emigration, and were troubled by it. The establishment of a second Muslim community would be a great threat, especially if they were able to establish an alliance with as significant a ruler as the Negus. They therefore sent a delegation of two emissaries, Amr ibn al-As and Abdullah ibn Rabiah, to persuade the Negus to send the Muslims back to Mecca. Initially they hoped he might do so without even hearing their case, but this was not to be.

The Negus summoned both parties. The Muslims chose Jafar ibn Abi Talib as their spokesperson. He explained to the Negus the basic teachings of Islam, and their experience of persecution in Mecca. He emphasized the Islamic belief in one God, rejection of idols, the injunction to respect kinship ties, speak truthfully, and oppose injustice. Jafar added that it was because of this teaching that the Muslims were experiencing persecution, and so they had sought protection in Abyssinia. Jafar also recited a portion of *surah Maryam*, the chapter of the Qur'an which teaches about the birth of Jesus.

Ramadan offers the following translation of the relevant portion:

> Relate in the Book [the story of] Mary, when she withdrew from her family to a place in the East. She placed a screen [to screen herself] from them: then when We sent to her our angel, and he appeared to her as a man in all respects. She said: 'I seek refuge from you in the shelter of the Most Gracious, if you fear Him.' He said: 'I am only a messenger from your Lord [to announce] to you

12. Ramadan, *In the Footsteps*, 59–62.

the gift of a pure son.' She said, 'How shall I have a son, seeing that no man has touched me, and that I am not unchaste?' He said: 'So [it will be]; your Lord says: "That is easy for Me and [We wish] to appoint him as a sign to men and a mercy from Us:" it is a matter decreed.'[13]

The Negus favorably received this reference to Jesus' virgin birth and he was inclined to grant the Muslims' request for asylum. However Amr and Abdullah were not finished yet. They spoke with the Negus privately, suggesting that Muslim beliefs about Jesus were not as similar to Christian ones as the Negus had first thought. The Negus, desiring clarification, summoned Jafar and his delegation a second time, demanding further information about what Muhammad taught about Jesus. This placed the Muslims in a difficult situation. Should they fudge the issue, to ensure security, or speak clearly, and risk expulsion and a return to Mecca, which would almost certainly lead to death for at least some of them?

Jafar resolved to be truthful. The Negus asked him what Muslims believed about Jesus, son of Mary. He responded:

> We say what our Prophet has taught us: he is God's servant, His messenger, His Spirit, His Word that he breathed into Mary, the Holy Virgin.[14]

Although there was no reference to Jesus as Son of God, there was enough to satisfy the Negus, who reportedly took a stick and exclaimed, "Jesus, son of Mary, does not exceed what you have said by the length of this stick." This conflation of theological positions surprised the Negus' religious advisors, but their concerns were ignored, the Muslims were granted asylum, and the Qurayshi delegation was sent back to Mecca. Jafar and his community were able to remain in Abyssinia for as long as they chose; they were welcomed and protected, despite the differences between their beliefs and Christian ones.

If this episode is thought of as a clear example of living in *dar al-shahada*, then what exactly does it teach? It could be held up as a model of how different religious groups can co-exist peacefully. However the story does not end there. Ramadan concludes the story by noting that the Negus converted to Islam and "remained in continuous contact with the Prophet Muhammad. He represented the latter at a wedding ceremony, and the

---

13. Ibid., 60–1.
14. Ibid., 61.

Prophet performed the prayer for the absent dead (*salat al-ghaib*) when he learned of the Negus' death."[15] The Negus did not remain a Christian, but once he encountered Islam, he became a Muslim, and so the story is not of two faiths co-existing peacefully, but an encounter between two faiths leading to conversion from one faith to another.

In the light of the Negus' conversion to Islam, it is therefore difficult to argue that the first *hijrah* from Mecca to Abyssinia is simply an example of peaceful co-existence in a multi-faith context. Rather it is a further example of the rapid growth of Islam in the first decades of its existence. The historical reality cannot be denied, but it is not really just an example of different faiths co-existing peacefully and respectfully together. If living in *dar al-shahada* includes the expectation that all those who encounter Islamic witness will convert to Islam, then it is not a suitable mode of existence for a pluralistic context. Ramadan does not make an explicit statement about this either in his account of the Negus or in his discussion of *dar al-shahada*, but it is an important point of clarification. Does *dar al-shahada* presume eventual conversion to Islam?

In his discussion as to whether Christians and Muslims worship the same God, the Protestant theologian Miroslav Volf develops his argument that it is possible to be simultaneously religiously exclusivist and politically pluralist.[16] There are, of course, many examples of societies that have been both religiously and politically exclusivist. Volf suggests that the sixteenth-century Christian principle *Cuius regio, eius religio* (the religion of the ruler is the religion of the people) is one example, and that the Muslim idea of *dhimmi*, whereby a non-Muslim subject in a Muslim state enjoys protection but not equal rights, is another. Arguably, the example of the conversion of the Negus makes that also an example of both religious and political exclusivism. But this does not mean that religious exclusivism necessarily leads to political exclusivism.

Volf suggests two basic conditions that are necessary for political pluralism: that the state is impartial in its treatment of all religions, and that each religion is allowed to bring its own understanding of the good life into the public arena. He further proposes that Muslim and Christian monotheism both share two common assumptions that promote political pluralism. These are, first, a belief in the ethical dimension of religious faith and, second, a belief that monotheism decoupled religion from the state

15. Ibid., 62.
16. Volf, *Allah*, 219–38.

and from ethnic belonging. Regarding the first point, justice, law, and freedom are all essential components of Abrahamic monotheism, and love of neighbor is so enshrined in their teaching to the extent that love of others is a manifestation of love of God. Regarding the second point, salvation is not the same as membership of a particular state or ethnic group. Granted, both Christians and Muslims consider themselves to be a universal group, but this is one that transcends all other ties. These two points lead Volf to suggest:

> Since religion is not identical with the state, and since doing justice and loving all neighbors is a religious duty, we must affirm (1) the appropriateness of there being more than one religion in a given state as well as (2) the right of each religious group to pursue its own religious vision of the good life.[17]

Ultimately, a religious exclusivist can also be politically pluralist because of a belief that God relates to all people on equal terms, that love of neighbor necessarily demands freedom of religion, and a refusal to coerce in matters of faith. Does Ramadan's vision of *dar al-shahada* embrace this understanding? A recent publication suggests it probably does.

In 2010, Ramadan published *The Quest for Meaning: Developing a Philosophy of Pluralism*. It is remarkably different from most of his previously published works. Most of his writings have tended to focus primarily on Islam, in particular on how Muslims can live an authentic life of faith in the twenty-first century West. These books suggest that Ramadan is religiously exclusivist, understanding Islam to be *the* true path. But *The Quest for Meaning* has a remarkably different tone. It does not promise certainty or clear answers in the quest, but it is a search for commonality and the universal. This does not mean religious pluralism, because for Ramadan the aim is not integration leading to the elimination of difference, but the elucidation of "spaces of intersection where we can meet on equal terms."[18]

The quest for spaces of intersection requires knowledge of the other. Ramadan is clear that isolation is not an option, arguing that we cannot simply remain theoretically opposed to Islamophobia whilst not knowing any Muslims personally. Rather we must "free ourselves from the ghetto of our noble, secure mind in order to enter the world of raw, tenacious, and sometimes mad and dangerous emotions."[19] Encounters with those who

17. Ibid., 230.
18. Ramadan, *The Quest for Meaning*, 24.
19. Ibid., 41.

are very different from myself does, of course, ultimately also become an encounter with myself. It is only as I engage with differences that I come to realize what I myself am like.

The expectations of *The Quest for Meaning* appear to be those of a religious exclusivist who is also politically pluralist. Ramadan expresses similar sentiments elsewhere, arguing that a committed Christian or Jew cannot be expected to compromise all they believe in order to work together with a Muslim.[20] Provided that there is freedom of religious belief, and individuals are able to enter and leave a religion as they personally see fit, then I am persuaded that *dar al-shahada* is arguably appropriate for life in twenty-first century Britain. But if there is an expectation of conversion, or of Islamic primacy, then this is no longer the case.

The final point of my argument is to develop an appropriate ethic for witness, for which I will rely heavily on Thiessen's book *The Ethics of Evangelism*, who uses the term proselytizing, which I will employ in this section, understanding it in similar terms to witness as an expression of faith that expects a positive response from those who encounter it. Some attempts at proselytizing are decidedly unethical, especially those that offer material inducements to conversion, or employ any form of physical, emotional, or social coercion. But unethical proselytizing does not necessarily preclude all attempts at proselytizing. Proselytizing is different from dialogue, as the latter does not expect conversion, while the former at least allows for the possibility. Both should be allowed—and expected—in a politically pluralist society. I suggest that, provided the fifteen criteria developed by Thiessen are adhered to, proselytizing will not conflict with a politically pluralistic society. These criteria are:

1. **Dignity:** The dignity of the person(s) being proselytized is protected;
2. **Care:** Ethical proselytizing is an expression of concern for the physical, social, economic, intellectual, emotional and spiritual needs of the person;
3. **Physical coercion:** Physical coercion in any form is prohibited;
4. **Psychological coercion:** Psychological coercion in any form is prohibited;
5. **Social coercion:** Whilst some degree of power is integral to proselytizing, power imbalances must not be exploited in any way;

20. Ramadan, *Islam, the West and the Challenge of Modernity*, 186.

6. **Inducement:** There should be no inducements offered to entice conversion. Where medical or humanitarian aid is offered by a faith based organization, every effort must be made to ensure it is possible for individuals to accept the aid without any expectation of conversion as a result;

7. **Rationality:** Proselytizing must allow for the functioning of human reason;

8. **Truthfulness:** The truth must be spoken about the religion being advocated and about other religions. Hidden agendas, deception, or hidden identities are immoral;

9. **Humility:** Proselytizing must be characterized by humility;

10. **Tolerance:** Those who hold different beliefs must be treated with love and respect. Differences can be acknowledged, but without insult or hostility;

11. **Motivation:** The primary motivation should be love for humanity that flows from a love for God;

12. **Identity:** The identity of the individual and their position in society must be respected;

13. **Cultural sensitivity:** The distinction between culture and religion is recognized and respected;

14. **Results:** Results are a by-product, not a central goal;

15. **Golden Rule:** Those who engage in ethical proselytizing assume the other has the right to proselytize as well.

If these fifteen criteria are central to *dar al-shahada*, the place of witness, then I suggest it can be integral to modern British society. I will close with a discussion of how this is arguably the case. Although Ramadan does not explicitly discuss Thiessen's criteria, nevertheless, his attitude does support them. This is perhaps seen most clearly in his discussion of *dar al-shahada* in a short book outlining the central tenets of his own beliefs, in which Ramadan states:

> The witness is no longer a stranger in the other's world, neither is he linked to the other by a contract: he is at home, among his own kind, and he simply tries to be consistent with his beliefs and in harmony with the people with whom he lives and builds his future.[21]

21. Ramadan, *What I Believe*, 52.

Ramadan's understanding of *dar al-shahada* therefore includes full commitment to Islam but at the same time also fully commitment to sharing public space. Ramadan elsewhere supports this with his argument that education should touch the heart and mind, enabling personal growth and autonomous decision making.[22] He subsequently develops arguments in favor of seven key rights, to life, to family, to housing, to education, to work, to justice and to solidarity, stressing in the discussion of this final right that every individual is responsible for participating actively in the society in which they live.[23] Two final examples will clarify the point further.

In his discussion of what he believes, Ramadan outlines seven key areas where he believes Muslims should develop.[24] They all begin with "c." The first is *confidence*, in self and in others. This, he suggests, must be associated with *consistency*, which includes the application of critical faculties to one's own beliefs, to ensure Islamic praxis matches Islamic teaching. Third, there must be a *contribution* to wider society, in particular to the welfare of the poor, the sick and the oppressed. Moreover, Muslims should recapture energy for *creativity* and rediscover a desire for initiative and risk taking. There is a need for *communication*, both within the Muslim community, and with other groups as well. Muslims must be unafraid to *contest*, to confront powers, governments and laws that are unjust stemming from a deep-seated *compassion* for the whole world and the needs of others. Someone who has made these seven criteria central to her behavior is unlikely to engage in unethical witness.

The same is true of anyone who is deeply motivated by forgiveness. Ramadan discusses the centrality of forgiveness in the major religions, and includes a personal story of an individual he learnt to forgive.[25] One of his students, Thierry, had grown up in a house where violence was the norm, and one day reacted violently towards his own mother. Initially, Ramadan was angry with Thierry, but once he understood the complexity of Thierry's circumstances, was able to understand and to forgive him for his actions. He explains his understanding of forgiveness as "an active human commitment to reforming and transforming ourselves,"[26] suggesting that people

---

22. Ramadan, *Western Muslims*, 129.
23. Ibid., 149–52.
24. Ramadan, *What I believe*, 87–9.
25. Ramadan, *The Quest for Meaning*, 201–4.
26. Ibid., 204.

are to be loved, but that a loving encounter, an encounter of witness, does not leave either individual unchanged.

Christians can find much in common with this complex and multifaceted idea of the *dar al-shahada*. We are called to be a community which witnesses to the truth of our faith in Jesus and the transforming power of the Holy Spirit, working for the good of others, caring for their needs, and also inviting them to come to faith in Jesus. Thus Rawlings argues that we can build cohesive communities whilst at the same time seeking conversion.[27] Honest and clear relationships are key. I am very close to some of my Muslim friends, and I know that they would love to see me become a Muslim, just as I would love them to become Christians. We have even said that to each other, and our relationship has been strengthened by that honesty.

Christians must also be clear about how they understand the term "witness," which is arguably distinct from the Muslim understanding. The gospels contain numerous instances of Jesus testifying or witnessing to the truth of his teaching (for example John 5:31–37; 8:14, 18) and his ultimate witness to the truth of his mission is his death and resurrection. The examples of Jesus, Paul, and Stephen, to pick three New Testament examples, suggest Christian discipleship is a life in which suffering and rejection are the likely norms. For a Christian, then, a life of witness always has the possibility of "red" or "bloody" martyrdom latent within it, since the Christian way is that of the cross.[28] While the liminal ritual of Islam is the declaration of the *shahada*, for Christians the liminal ritual is baptism, which is a sign of incorporation into the death and resurrection of Jesus (Romans 6:3–5). Christian witness is distinct from Islamic witness, and we must understand this difference as we look for areas of common ground.

## WHAT KIND OF FRIENDSHIP?

Christians are called to be confident witnesses to our faith in Jesus Christ, but not to be coercive in how we do so. We must recognize the complexity of our own identity and the complexity of the society in which we live. We are to be clear of our own faith, and on the basis of that clarity recognize that there is much that we can learn from our Muslim brothers and sisters, and their faith offers challenges to our own practices, as subsequent chapters will show.

27. Rawlings, *Engaging with Muslims*.
28. Jensen, *Martyrdom and Identity*, 5–6.

# 3

# The Four Practical Pillars

THE PREVIOUS CHAPTER FOCUSED on the first pillar of Islam, the *shahada*, the declaration of faith in God and Mohammad as his messenger. I will now move on to what Ramadan terms the four "practical" pillars.[1] These are *salah* (ritual prayer); *zakat* (financial giving); *sawn* (fasting) and *hajj* (pilgrimage). Before examining them in detail, I will first discuss the general context of Muslim religious observance including the basic orientation within Islam towards permission rather than prohibition and the central functions of the pillars within Islam.

## MUSLIM RELIGIOUS OBSERVANCE

Much as there are many nominal Christians, there are also large numbers of nominal Muslims, individuals who self-define as Muslims but are not rigorous in practicing all the requirements of their faith. Ramadan estimated that in the West at least four out of every five Muslims do not practice their religion regularly, and so, for example, do not say their prayers every day.[2] He further suggests that less than two in five attend the Friday gathering at the mosque. More recently he goes into further detail regarding this eighty percent, proposing that for most, the label "Muslim" is as much cultural as

---

1. Ramadan, *Western Muslims*, 120.
2. Ramadan, *To be a European Muslim*, 121.

religious, meaning they abstain from alcohol and pork, observe the month-long Ramadan fast "out of faith or family (and/or) cultural tradition," but that is all.[3] Others within this group may not even be this observant, and might define themselves as atheistic, agnostic, although there is, of course, a difference between a Muslim atheist and a Christian atheist, in that it is a different god that they do not believe in. Of the one-in-five Muslims who is observant and diligent in practicing faith, those who were born and raised in the UK may also have reformist approaches to Islam, looking to practice Islam in a way that is compatible with contemporary life. The focus of Ramadan's (and hence my) discussion is on this twenty percent: those who take their faith seriously but also wish to live as active British citizens. This is the focus of much of Ramadan's writing: what does it mean to be a British Muslim today?

## Permission not Prohibition

Before discussing the obligations incumbent on observant Muslims, I will set out expectations regarding religious praxis within Islam, which are permission giving rather than prohibitive. Ramadan is clear that it "is a fundamental rule in Islam to assert the priority of permission," and further that "freedom and innocence are the first states of man in an open world." He summarizes his point that "The field of prohibition is very restrained in comparison to the horizon of what is possible."[4] The shift from "field" to "horizon" is an instructive metaphor: there are clear restrictions, actions, and attitudes that are expressly forbidden in Islam, demarcated within a closed field. But, Ramadan argues, these are very minor compared with the wealth of possibilities in the service of God, that are suggested by the open horizon of the faithful searching to live for God in the world.

The experience of Adam and Eve is instructive here. The Qur'an makes clear a statement of generous permission and very limited prohibition:

> And We said, 'Adam! Inhabit the Garden, you and your wife, and eat freely of it wherever you please, but do not go near this tree, or you will both be evildoers.' Then Satan caused them both to slip from there, and to go out from where they were. And We said, 'Go down, some of you an enemy to others! The earth is a dwelling place for you, and enjoyment (of life) for a time.' Then Adam

---

3. Ramadan, *What I Believe*, 46.
4. Ramadan, *Islam, the West and the Challenge of Modernity*, 19–20.

received certain words from his Lord, and He turned to him (in forgiveness). Surely He—He is the One who turns (in forgiveness), the Compassionate. (2:35-7)[5]

As in the Christian understanding of Genesis 3, Adam and Eve are given freedom in the Garden of Eden, with the one exception of the tree from which they are forbidden to eat. But Satan causes them to stumble, and they succumb to the temptation to take what is prohibited, and so are expelled from the Garden. But there is then a crucial difference: in the Qur'anic account, Adam is forgiven his sin, and so there is no doctrine of original sin (or inherited corruption as some like to term it). In the Islamic understanding, human beings are born pure, and are not accountable to God until they reach the age of responsibility, normally understood to be puberty. Elsewhere, Ramadan quotes the Prophet as regarding children as wholly belonging to God, and being presumed innocent.[6] This crucial doctrinal difference is key for understanding the place of praxis within Islam and Christianity. In the Christian understanding of salvation of sinners through the grace of God, anything we do is a response of love but cannot be instrumental in earning our salvation. But in Islam, those who are born innocent, as they mature to adulthood are then held responsible for their actions, and can, by their own merit, earn the forgiveness and favor of God through diligent prayer and obedient faith, although one can never be certain of one's fate, and any Muslim will say that their eternal destiny is ultimately dependent on the mercy of Allah. There is within Islam a five-stage scheme of permission, which ranges from obligation (*wajib*) to recommended or preferable (*musahab, mandub*), through permissible (*mubah*), to reprehensible (*makruh*) and prohibited (*haram*) behavior, rather than just the simpler black-and-white contrast between permitted and prohibited (*al-halal wal-haram*) that is often cited. Human beings always have a range of choices available to them.

Ramadan is clear that human beings are born innocent, and that successive revelations of God marked the way (*shariah*) that they are to follow.[7] Prohibition is to be regarded as both limiting and orientating, that is to say it both restrains and also directs focus for godly living. There are, of course, areas of doubt, about which the guidance of learned scholars could be sought. Ramadan suggests a volume by Yusuf al-Qaradawi, *The Lawful*

5. Quotations of the Qur'an are from Droge *The Qur'an*.
6. Ramadan, *In the Footsteps*, 213-4.
7. Ramadan, *Islam, the West and the Challenge of Modernity*, 21.

*and the Prohibited in Islam*, which gives detailed advice on a range of areas of daily life, including food, clothing, family, and social relations, but concludes that the best advice is simply to avoid such problematic areas, a suggestion that sows some seeds of doubt as to the width of the horizon of the possible. To summarize: everything that has not been clearly prohibited by God is permitted, but where doubts remain, the best thing to do is simply steer clear of such areas (and so presume prohibition).

## The Function of the Pillars

Throughout his writing, Ramadan regularly returns to two key emphases for the five pillars of Islam: community and purification. It is important to recognize that none of the pillars can be observed alone, but all are, by their very nature, communal actions. The *shahada* must be said in the presence of two witnesses; prayer is best done in community; giving of necessity involves, at the very least, benefactor and recipient; fasting reminds one of the needs of others, and is itself a community activity; and pilgrimage is also done in company, not alone. There is therefore no real place within Islam for the solitary hermit who withdraws from the world. As Ramadan explains: being an observant Muslim means participation in the social order, a fact that becomes very evident as he discusses each of the four practical pillars.[8]

Second, the pillars are means of purification and re-orientation of the self.[9] This works on a number of levels. The pillars demand that one remembers God and one's obligations towards him. They demand management of time: the prayers on a daily basis, fasting, and giving on an annual basis, and the obligation to pilgrimage to Mecca once in a lifetime can radically shape the direction of an individual's entire life. The communal nature of the actions also mitigate against self-absorption, and towards community life. The pillars are, he is clear, the means, not an end in themselves. Nevertheless, if observed, "They are the indispensible and essential arbiter for mastering our inward and outward life so as to be totally and perpetually imbibed by Faith and its light."[10]

To summarize, Ramadan argues that the pillars are of little merit in and of themselves, but at the same time, they are the essential foundations

---

8. Ramadan, *Islam, the West*, 39.
9. Ramadan, *Western Muslims*, 120.
10. Ramadan, *To be a European Muslim*, 20.

## The Four Practical Pillars

upon which the house of faith is built. They remind Muslims they are not isolated individuals, but part of a much wider community, and this is perhaps clearest in the ritual of communal prayer.

### SALAH (RITUAL PRAYER)

I have deliberately translated *salah* as "ritual prayer" in order to give recognition to the tradition of *duah*, or free prayer, within Islam. While the observance of *salah* is carefully proscribed, there are no such clear instructions for free prayer, which Muslims will also engage in. The stereotype of Islamic prayer as being entirely wooden is inaccurate, although formal prayer is by far the most dominant form, and is the type of prayer considered here.

There were successive stages in the revelation of ritual prayer to the Prophet. Ramadan records that Muhammad received a visit from the Angel Gabriel, who taught him how to perform ablutions and practice ritual prayer, based on recitation of the Qur'an and a precise, cyclical series of gestures (*raka*).[11] Initially prayer was performed twice a day, in the morning and the evening, and only later in Muhammad's lifetime came to be carried out five times a day. Two other aspects of the successive revelation of how *salah* should be practiced are also worth noting: the development of the call to prayer, and the shift in direction of prayer.

The call to prayer was not something initially suggested by Muhammad himself. Rather, Abdullah ibd Zayd, "an Ansar who had taken part in the second covenant of al-Aqabah, came to him and told him of a dream in which a man taught him the manner in which he was to call others to prayer."[12] Muhammad decided this was a genuine revelation of God, and entrusted the duty of calling others to prayer to Bilal, a former slave. The call has remained unchanging down the generations, affirming the greatness of God, professing faith in God and Muhammad as the Messenger of God, and inviting others to come and pray. Initially Muslims prayed facing Jerusalem; but some eighteen months after persecution had forced the first believers from Mecca to Medina, the direction of their prayers was shifted to Mecca, and specifically the *Ka'aba* within Mecca.

This account of the development of *salah* as practiced today is important for understanding that, although the form is now fixed, it was not so

---

11. Ramadan, *In the Footsteps*, 42.
12. Ibid., 92.

static in the first days of Islam. One especially notable difference is that in the early days of Islam, men and women prayed together in the mosque in Medina. Ramadan explains that women would line up to pray behind men, "as the posture of prayer, in its various stages, requires an arrangement that preserves modesty, decency and respect."[13] Although this was the original practice, it is no longer observed: men and women now pray separately, and British mosques have very limited facilities for women, if they have any facilities at all. I will examine Ramadan's discussion of the place of women in Islam in a separate chapter, and so will not deal with the issue here, but nevertheless wish to recognize that shared prayer is an important piece of Islamic history that is, sadly, often overlooked.

Ramadan is clear that prayer is very much a communal action. I have found two places where he quotes a saying of Muhammad that prayer in community is twenty-seven times more efficacious than prayer alone.[14] I find this specific number quite curious. Am I to take this to mean "much more," as Jesus' instruction to Peter that he should forgive up to seventy times seven (Matthew 18:22)? Or is it a precise calculation, part of how Allah will weigh the good and bad deeds of sinners at the judgment? Ramadan nowhere explains, but my inclination is that perhaps it is the latter, and conversations with Muslim friends support this hunch. The basic point is therefore that prayer should not be done alone: the link between God, whilst personal, is more corporate than individual, and prayer should be carried out in the context of a formally gathered congregation, which must consist of a minimum of four people.

As a Christian reading Ramadan, I am left with a number of questions regarding the Muslim practice of prayer. The first I have already hinted at, and concerns the separation of genders, to the point of exclusion of women from many British mosques. There is an often cited *hadith* which implies it is better for women to pray at home than in a mosque, and this is used to defend the lack of women's facilities in many mosques. While I recognize the importance of focus on prayer and the elimination of distraction, I find it hard to understand why more adequate provision is not made for women to be able to pray together, either in a separate room, or at the back of main prayer halls. Christianity has often treated women badly, and in many cultures even today, men and women sit separately in church, but at least

---

13. Ibid., 148.
14. Ramadan, *To be a European Muslim*, 156; *Western Muslims*, 88.

they are permitted to enter the same building, a right that is not enjoyed by all Muslim women.

A second question concerns the greater power of corporate prayer. Jesus reminded us that when we gather he is present with us (Matthew 18:20). It is noticeable that this promise of Jesus refers to any gathering of two or three believers, "not a formally convened ecclesiastical council"[15] or official congregational gathering, implying a less formal approach to corporate prayer in Christianity than in Islam. Jesus' instructions on prayer are often addressed corporately, as are Paul's, suggesting while it may be less formally organized than in Islam, corporate prayer is an important element of Christian faith and practice. English does not, unfortunately, distinguish between a singular and plural "you," and so this fact is easily obscured in English Bibles. Whilst I recognize the power of corporate prayer, I also heed the instruction, addressed to individuals, to go into an inner room, close the door, and pray in secret, so that my heavenly Father, who hears in secret, can reward me (Matthew 6:6). Christians should pray both together and alone; neglecting either is detrimental to our faith.

A related point concerns the balance of structure and freedom. A rigid framework can both constrain and guide: how does one guard against the danger of simply going through the motions? Speaking through Amos, the Lord is clear in his abhorrence of empty ritual at the expense of righteous living (5:21–4) and I wonder how one guards against the practice of five daily prayers becoming an empty ritual? There is, of course, great value in having a set form of prayer, and I know I have found the discipline of the set prayers of the Anglican daily office invaluable for keeping my prayer life alive when it has faltered. But I am also keenly aware of the freedom of spontaneous prayer. Islam does, as I mentioned above, have the tradition of *duah*, but it does not seem to be as referenced by Ramadan as one might expect, given his central aim of encouraging devout and thinking Muslims to practice their faith in Britain in the twenty-first century. When discussing other issues, for example *halal* food, Ramadan is very critical of overly literalistic and wooden interpretations, but I am not aware of his mentioning even the possibility that prayer could ever become this. Perhaps it never has for him, in which case he is truly blessed. I am left challenged by the frequency with which a devout Muslim prays, but also questioning how to make such regular, formal prayer a living part of a vibrant faith, and not simply an empty ritual.

15. France, *Matthew*, 698.

## What Kind of Friendship?

## ZAKAT (FINANCIAL GIVING)

The expectations related to *zakat* are quite different from Christian understandings of giving, and are worth setting out in detail. *Zakat* does not refer to charitable giving, but to the systematic giving of 2.5 percent of one's wealth each year to the poor. Only certain items are eligible for *zakat*, namely: gold, silver, cash, and any stock purchased for trade. Personal items, such as one's home or clothing are not considered. Furthermore, only sane adult Muslims who possess wealth above a certain minimum threshold, the *nisab*, for one whole lunar year are obliged to pay *zakat*. There is some dispute amongst Muslims regarding the precise value of the *nisab*, which is calculated as the value of a set weight of both silver and gold. The amount for silver is 612.36 grams (52.2 *tola*) and 87.48 grams (7.5 *tola*) of gold. Muslim Aid's online *zakat* calculator values this for 2015 as £247 ($381) in silver and £2279 ($3516) in gold, and suggests that since silver was used as the standard in the time of Muhammad, it should still be used today, even though the value of silver has fallen considerably since the seventh century.[16] There are also rules regarding the recipients, who must be sufficiently poor that they themselves do not possess the *nisab*. Furthermore, the recipients must become owners of the *zakat* themselves: hence giving to general appeals, for example supporting a hospital trust, does not count as paying *zakat*. To summarize, *zakat* is a tax on one's surplus wealth, which should be given annually to individual recipients who are sufficiently poor to merit such generosity. It is possible to give to charitable organizations, but they must ensure all of the *zakat* goes to individual recipients, and not to cover their own costs.

I have included all this detail to illustrate both the complexity of the system and the relatively modest amounts concerned. Many of an individual's possessions are exempted, and the amount required to be paid on what is eligible is quite modest. The process of calculating how much of one's income is liable for *zakat* is complex, and there are online *zakat* calculators to help individuals work out what they owe.[17] What is striking is that they all have slight variations in their calculations of the *nisab*, suggesting there is no complete agreement as to its value.

---

16. https://www.muslimaid.org/zakat-calculator/. Values correct as of February 2015.

17. In addition to Muslim Aid's, others can be found at http://www.islamic-relief.org/zakat/zakat-calculator/ and http://zakatcalculator.co.uk/.

## The Four Practical Pillars

Ramadan does not touch on the technicalities of calculating *zakat*, but rather on the moral issues that are beneath the surface. He notes that all economic actions, whether related to production or consumption, have moral implications, describes *zakat* as the third pillar of Islam and suggests, "Its essence pinpoints the importance of social participation in the Muslim universe."[18] While *zakat* is in one sense a simple tax on wealth, it should be understood primarily as a religious obligation, one that seeks to restore some sort of balance of wealth between those who have and those who do not. It is not simply a question of personal goodness, but of social justice; hence Abu Bakr, the first successor to Muhammad, was prepared to fight the tribes of the south when they refused to pay their *zakat*.

Ramadan identifies four dimensions to personal spending, which relate closely to obligations to pay *zakat*. These are giving to please God; giving in right measure; giving to fight egoism and hoarding; and the need to display caution when giving.[19]

First giving should be done to please God and donation carried out for his sake. Thus the Qur'an states:

> The parable of those who contribute their wealth in the way of God is like the parable of a grain of corn that grows seven ears: in each ear (there are) a hundred grains. (So) God doubles for whomever He pleases. God is embracing, knowing. . . . But the parable of those who contribute their wealth, seeking the approval of God and confirmation for themselves, is like the parable of a garden on a hill. A heavy rain smites it, and it yields its produce twofold. And if a heavy rain does not smite it, a shower (does). God sees what you do. (2:261, 265).

Ramadan suggests that Muslims give because they are aware of divine knowledge and observation of their lives; Allah knows the intentions of the giver and the spender of money. Hence devout Muslims will not simply give *zakat*, but will be found "donating again and again of our surplus in order to live according to our rights in unity with the rights of others."[20]

Second, while the desire to please God will encourage one to give, it should be in right measure. Ramadan is clear that Muslims are under no obligation to live as hermits; or give everything away, stating "It cannot

---

18. Ramadan, *Islam, the West and the Challenge of Modernity*, 139.
19. Ramadan, *To be a European Muslim*, 178–82; *Islam, the West*, 141–3.
20. Ramadan, *Islam, the West*, 141.

be a question of impoverishing oneself in order to render justice."[21] Each Muslim must reach the appropriate level of donation, guided by the Qur'an:

> Do not keep your hand chained to your neck, nor extend it all the way, or you will sit down blamed (and) impoverished. . . . And (they are) those who, when they contribute, are neither wanton nor stingy, but right between that. (17:29; 25:67).

The expectation, Ramadan indicates, is therefore of sensible generosity. There are duties incumbent upon Muslims, expectations they are bound to meet in caring for their family, their fellow believers, and all humanity. But there is not an expectation that they will give excessively, or at undue cost to themselves.

Third, Ramadan suggests giving is a way of fighting against egoism and hoarding. The annual practice of calculating one's wealth and then giving away a set portion of it is a deliberate counter to self-absorption, and forgetfulness of God. The Qur'an has clear warnings on the danger of keeping one's wealth entirely for oneself:

> Those who hoard the gold and the silver, and do not spend it in the way of God—give them news of a painful punishment. On the day when it will be heated in the Fire of Gehenna, and their foreheads and their sides and their backs will be branded with it: "This is what you have hoarded for yourselves, so taste what you have hoarded!" (9:34–35).

Accumulated wealth that has not been subject to *zakat* thus becomes the very instrument of divine punishment of those whose over-obsession with their valuables has taken them away from remembrance of their God. The discipline of giving is thus central to an active life of faith. A devout Muslim will not simply give *zakat*, but also *sadaqah* (voluntary charity, given out of compassion and love to any worthy recipient) and *lillah*, (literally, "for Allah," extra voluntary giving over and above *zakat*, specifically for Islamic causes).

Fourth, there is an expectation that giving will be done cautiously, or even secretly (although Ramadan does not use this phrase). Although giving reminds one of the needs of others, it is essentially a private action that should be done primarily for the sight of God, not of other people. Caution is important to preserve the dignity of those who are recipients of

---

21. Ibid., 141.

## The Four Practical Pillars

one's *zakat*, because the very act of giving to them indicates their poverty. Thus the Qur'an states:

> If you make freewill offerings publicly, that is excellent, but if you hide it and give it to the poor, that is better for you, and will absolve you of some of your evil deeds. God is aware of what you do. (2:271).

The concern is thus to prevent social embarrassment, to give even before the poor ask for help. The giver will receive a suitable reward from Allah.

Ramadan concludes his discussion of personal giving with a reminder of the social dimensions of the action. In his view, if one possesses material goods, one is necessarily obliged towards generous giving. One cannot shamelessly increase one's own wealth at the price of exploiting others. Human beings are free and able to make their own choices, but they are also morally accountable before both God and their fellow human beings, and must use their wealth wisely.

In response to my reading of Ramadan, I will make two observations relating to the obligation to give financially. First, I am struck the amount one is expected to give. My understanding of Christian giving is that it should be sacrificial. Jesus commends the Pharisees for tithing their herbs, but also demands of them weightier sacrificial actions in defense of justice and mercy (Luke 11:42). Whilst there are set amounts in the Old Testament, the New Testament nowhere sets a figure for how much Christians give. Paul expects Christian giving to result in equality for all believers (2 Corinthians 8:13), and the only people Jesus commends for giving financially are the widow who gives everything to the Temple (Mark 12:43-4; Luke 21:3-4) and Zacchaeus when he gives away half of his wealth and repays those whom he has defrauded four times what he stole (Luke 19:8). Zacchaeus' actions may have impoverished him; they certainly greatly reduced his wealth. Similarly, the rich young ruler is told to sell all he has and give to the poor (Matthew 19:21; Mark 10:21; Luke 18:22). An obligation to give a mere two and a half percent of one's non-essential assets is a much smaller demand than that made by the New Testament.

It is certainly true that very few Christians have taken the obligation to give as seriously as some of the texts cited above imply they should. Paul is right in his observation to Timothy that "A love of money is the root of all kinds of evil" (1 Timothy 6:10). It is also true that many Muslims are incredibly generous, and give far more than the obligation of *zakat*, whilst many

Christians do not even approach this level of generosity. But my question is not related so much to praxis as to aspiration. Fundamentally, I am unsure if the obligation of *zakat* is a sufficient reminder that all I have is God's and I am simply called to steward it and give account of what I have been given at the last judgment, as the parable of the talents (Matthew 25:14–30) implies.

My second observation relates to the discipline of the annual calculation of wealth, and an obligation to give once one has made these calculations. It is generally a Muslim habit to engage in such calculations during the month of Ramadan, because it is believed that any good action performed during this month carries a greater reward. I am not in the habit of making such annual calculations, and on reading Ramadan have asked myself whether this might be a good habit to get into. When I moved jobs I calculated how much of my income I would give away, and whom to give it to (currently around seventeen percent of my pre-tax income, but my housing is provided with my job, so it is not quite as generous as it seems), and I do not review it annually, even though I receive small increases in my wages over time. Similarly, the vast majority of my giving is by direct bank transfer, with the intention of prioritizing giving over all other forms of spending, and being as tax efficient as possible. But the downside is that I do not often consciously think about giving, and perhaps to do so would be an important counter to the natural human tendency to hoard money for oneself.

There is much that I would commend in Ramadan's discussion of giving, especially the need to give in secret, and to give as a personal spiritual discipline, to remember the generosity of God and to fight against the self-absorption of sinful humanity curved inwards. But I remain unsure that giving should merely be from one's surplus. When Paul encourages the Corinthians to give, he cites the example of Christ (2 Corinthians 8:9), and if I take him as a model for my own giving, it must not just be from my surplus, but must be an act of dying to self and at the very least constrain my desires somehow, as the Spirit leads me.

## SAWN (FASTING)

Fasting during the month of Ramadan is primarily an annual process of reorientation and re-focus. A devout Muslim will fast during the hours of daylight (defined as when there is sufficient light to distinguish between a white thread and a black thread) for the entirety of the lunar month of

## The Four Practical Pillars

Ramadan. Fasting is not simply from food, but also from all drinks and any sexual activity. Traditionally the fast is broken by eating a single date, before praying together, and then returning home for a meal. Since they are based on a lunar calendar, the dates for Ramadan shift slightly each year in the Gregorian solar calendar, and when they fall during the British summer, the hours of fasting are much longer in the UK than in Middle East. All healthy adult Muslims are expected to fast; those who are pregnant, ill, or too young are exempted, although many children will fast for at least some of the time, in order to gain familiarity with the discipline and build their capacity to fast.

Ramadan suggests that Muhammad was both rigorous in his own personal discipline of fasting, but also generous in his expectations of other people, encouraging his followers to be moderate, not extremist, in their personal religious practice.[22] Muhammad discouraged his followers from an overly austere lifestyle, speaking against complete chastity or continuous fasting, suggesting that moderation was better than overly zealous praxis. The following quote illustrates the point:

> Aishah reports that once a man came to the Prophet and told him: "I am lost!" When the Prophet asked why, the man confessed: "I had intercourse with my wife during the fasting hours of Ramadan." Muhammad answered, "Give charity!" The man replied, "I own nothing!" Then he sat down a short distance from the Prophet. Some time later, a man arrived, bringing a dish of food as a gift for Muhammad. The Prophet called out "Where is the man who is lost?" "Here," answered the first man, the one who had confessed his transgression. Muhammad told him, "Take this food and give it away in charity." In astonishment, the man cried, "To one poorer than myself? My family has nothing to eat!" "Well, then, eat it yourselves," the Prophet replied with a smile.[23]

Ramadan discusses fasting at some length, describing the month of Ramadan as "a school enabling the Muslim conscience to return to what is essential in the message, its objectives, and the questionings necessary to grasp higher goals."[24] He explains that this month entails a deliberate shift in the normal rhythm of life, breaking habits of consumption and indeed the whole daily routine. Fasting is at its heart a spiritual discipline, but it

---

22. Ramadan, *In the Footsteps*, 111–2.
23. Ibid., 113.
24. Ramadan, *Radical Reform*, 239.

also has an ethical dimension, demanding that believers question their choices and goals in life, and remember those who have little or nothing of their own. In Ramadan's view, this has been perverted, if not lost altogether.

In many Muslim majority countries, the month of Ramadan brings about a radical shift in how daily life is conducted, but this shift is not necessarily entirely spiritual. Many people simply become nocturnal, sleeping through much of the day, and staying awake through the night, and perhaps even consuming more than they normally do by attending nighttime Ramadan parties. Tariq Ramadan is scathing of such behavior, describing it as "formalist perversion: norm and form are maintained while the religious practice's ethical goals are lost."[25] Rightly practiced, fasting can be very beneficial for the believer, but if perverted, it ceases to have any real meaning.

The discipline required to fast throughout the month of Ramadan always challenges me, especially when it falls during the British summer: not eating or drinking for eighteen hours or more is a serious challenge, one that I am unsure I could complete for a whole month. I fast occasionally, but not that often, and whenever I talk with Muslims about their discipline of fasting, I wonder whether my own spiritual growth has suffered because I do not fast regularly. Although Tariq Ramadan only discusses the month-long Ramadan fast, there is also within Islam a spiritual discipline of fasting for single days throughout the year, either for particular occasions, or simply as a weekly discipline. I find this easier to identify with and understand, and so regard it as something I am more likely to try and emulate within my own spiritual life than the month long Ramadan fast.

The closest comparable Christian discipline to the Ramadan fast is the observance of Lent (and perhaps also Advent), but here there is no strong tradition of complete abstinence by day and consumption by night, but rather a reduction in consumption for a set period, which does itself continue. Different strands within Christianity take fasting more seriously than Western Protestantism, reminding me that this is an area in which I need to grow.

The main question I am left wrestling with is that of how to avoid legalism but at the same time to live a disciplined Christian life. I do not believe Christians are obligated to fast in the same way that Muslims are; certainly I do not think fasting is a means of earning God's favor, as I am convinced we are brought into and maintain our relationship with God by his grace, and through faith in his actions for us. But at the same time,

---

25. Ibid., 239.

## The Four Practical Pillars

I know Jesus assumes I will fast. His instructions for not disfiguring one's appearance presume that fasting is a normal spiritual discipline rather than an exceptional action (Matthew 6:16–8). The grace of God may mean I am not obligated to fast, but that same grace does expect a response from me, including one that denies the power consumerism tries to have over me.

Perhaps the problem that Ramadan identifies, that of "formalist perversion" is too deeply rooted within me. I live in a culture dominated by consumption, and have I let it take too much control over my own life? As with my discussion of Christian giving above, I do not believe one can set a clear rule for how often one should fast and what one should fast from. Paul expects believers who are married to sometimes fast from sexual activity in order to devote themselves to prayer (1 Corinthians 7:5). In recent times it has been common to talk, for example of a "carbon fast," where we try to consume less electricity or drive less. Similarly, we could fast from unnecessary consumption, from social media or from watching television. The discipline of fasting is primarily about reorientation and recognition of divine sovereignty. What is the Spirit guiding me to fast from?

## HAJJ (PILGRIMAGE)

Islam is a religion rooted in a particular geographic location in a way that Christianity is not. There is no comparable obligation in Christianity to the expectation that all Muslims who are able to will travel, at least once during their lives, to perform pilgrimage (*hajj*) in Mecca. Muslims who lack the financial means or the physical or mental capacity to make the journey are exempted, but the overwhelming majority of believers are expected to attempt the journey. The obligation is not simply to travel to Mecca whenever one is able, but to do so at a specific time of year: the 8th to 12th of the lunar month *Dhu Hijjah*, which culminates with the celebration of *Eid al-Adha*, the festival of sacrifice, the commemoration of the almost-sacrifice of Ishamael by Abraham.

The pilgrimages itself commemorates the final pilgrimage of Muhammad, and there are set rituals that all pilgrims must perform while on pilgrimage. All pilgrims wear the same white clothing, and abstain from sexual relations, and must ensure they do not argue with anyone or kill anything during their pilgrimage. Millions converge on Mecca for the week of the *hajj*. Each person performs *tawaf,* walking counter-clockwise seven times around the *Ka'aba*, the cube shaped building which is the central focus for *salah*. They also run back and forth seven times between the hills of Al-Safa and Al-Marwah and then drink water from the Zamzam well. This commemorates Hagar's search for, and God's provision of, water when she and her son Ishmael were abandoned in the desert. On the next day, pilgrims spend the day in vigil on the plains of Mount Arafat, reciting the Qur'an and then remaining in prayer near the place where Muhammad gave his final sermon. On the following day, pilgrims throw stones in a ritual stoning of the Devil, an act of remembrance of Abraham's temptation by the Devil when he was called by God to sacrifice Ishmael. Once this ritual has been completed, male pilgrims shave their heads (and female pilgrims cut their hair), and sacrifice a lamb or camel as an offering to begin the three-day celebration of *Eid al-Adha*. During those three days pilgrims will perform two further *tawaf*, and also the stoning ritual again.

Each year, millions perform *hajj*, and so the primary spiritual discipline that is incumbent upon all pilgrims is that of patience. Everything takes hours, and everywhere is very crowded. The pilgrimage should both deepen believers' personal spirituality and also remind them of the community of which they are part. One of the central messages of the *hajj* is of

> The absolute equality of human beings before God, regardless of race, social class, or gender, for the only thing that distinguishes them lies in what they do with themselves, with their intelligence, their qualities, and most of all their heart.[26]

There is a strong tradition of pilgrimage within certain strands of Christianity, but even where pilgrimage is central, it does not have a comparable role to the *hajj* in Islam. Christians of all traditions travel to particular places to encounter other believers, perhaps to remove themselves from the distractions of their daily routines and to get closer to God. Pilgrimage does not have to be understood as a journey to a specifically religious shrine, such as Walsingham in the UK. It might mean a week at a Christian conference, a quiet day of prayer and reflection, and much more.

For me, the question is whether this must be done in a particular way, or whether any pilgrimage will suffice. Christianity, like Islam, identifies itself as a global faith, and most Christians recognize that they have a lot to learn from other traditions and from travelling to places with the specific intention of growing in their relationship with God. I do not think there can be any obligation incumbent on Christians to select a particular place

---

26. Ramadan, *In the Footsteps*, 196–7.

or mode of travel and while I recognize the value in a single event that radically equalizes all believers, I also recognize that, from my personal conversations with a number of Muslims who have performed *hajj* themselves, commercial exploitation is as active here as in many other spheres of life. There are different packages for different pilgrims; those who pay more do stay in more comfortable accommodation and potentially get faster access to the different pilgrimage sites. I have not read anything in Ramadan's writing that specifically addresses this issue, but given his comments about fasting quoted above it seems likely that he would be equally critical of a subversion of the radical equality of the *hajj*.

## WHAT KIND OF FRIENDSHIP?

In this chapter I have briefly outlined something of the central understanding of Muslim religious observance in general and the four practical pillars of Islam in particular. Two common threads have emerged through all of my discussion, which I will summarize here. First, I recognize the challenge that the spiritually disciplined Muslim presents to many Christian believers, perhaps especially Protestants, who are keen to emphasize salvation by grace and not works. While I wholeheartedly endorse this desire to prioritize the work of God's grace in my life, it is important to remember Paul's injunction to continually work out our salvation with fear and trembling while God works in and through us according to his good purposes (Philippians 2:12–3). Equally, James (2:14–26) reminds us that faith without works is dead, and it is easy for an emphasis on grace to become lifeless. A disciplined life of regular prayer, committed giving, regular fasting, and pilgrimage has much to commend it and demonstrates a wholehearted response to the grace God has shown us in Jesus Christ.

My second point is in tension with the first. While I commend a disciplined life, I wish to avoid legalism. Christianity is not proscriptive of praxis in the way Islam is, and expects individual believers and communities of the faithful to work out what the Spirit is calling them to do both separately and together. We should not slip into the lazy habit of legalistic rules, but equally we must not let the lack of direct guidance excuse us from the hard work of responding to the Spirit's call. In our friendship with Muslims we can let their discipline sharpen our discipline, but also live out our experience of grace as a challenge and a witness to them.

# 4

# Steps for Social Engagement

RAMADAN RECOGNIZES THE DIVERSITY of religions in the world, arguing from an Islamic perspective that these are a test from Allah, which teach us how to manage difference. He suggests that the basis for engagement should be sincerity, honesty, and mutual respect.[1] He further argues that those who engage positively with Muslims should not be expected "to accept everything in Islam or of what the believers say."[2] He terms this a "realistic pluralism," which stresses cooperative action in response to common concerns. In a similar vein, Jonathan Chaplin argues for a Christian retrieval of multiculturalism, suggesting that it is quite possible to hold an exclusivist understanding of salvation whilst also wanting to support engagement with a diverse range of people.[3] In an earlier report, Chaplin refers to Rowan Williams' distinction between "programmatic" and "procedural" secularism:

> The former intentionally imposes a secularist faith on the public realm and works to privatize religious faith as much as possible, while the latter seeks to allow all faith perspectives equal access to the public realm but claims to confer no political privilege on any.[4]

1. Ramadan, *Western Muslims*, 202–8.
2. Ramadan, *Islam, the West and the Challenge of Modernity*, 186.
3. Chaplin, *Multiculturalism*.
4. Chaplin, *Talking God*, 21.

## Steps for Social Engagement

Although the terminology differs, and there are perhaps some technical differences between them, "realistic pluralism" and "procedural secularism" share the common cause of recognizing difference and simultaneously affirming a desire to work closely together. Having discussed religious obligations, the focus of my discussion shifts in this transitional chapter towards Ramadan's criteria for social engagement, building on the notion of *dar al-shahada* discussed earlier. I will examine three areas: a desire for respect, not tolerance; a move away from both assimilation and alienation; and the strategy of engagement Ramadan advocates.

### RESPECT, NOT TOLERANCE

Ramadan argues strongly against the notion of tolerance, and instead promotes the urgent necessity of developing mutual respect.[5] Tolerance, as he defines it, is a very limited virtue. An individual can be tolerated, but at the same time ignored. Furthermore, and more crucially, tolerance assumes an imbalance of power, as power-holders tolerate those weaker than them. Thus he describes tolerance as "intellectual charity on the part of the powerful."[6] Tolerance is therefore understood as a condescending welcome of a weaker person, a conditional welcome that perpetuates that weakened status.

In a similar vein, Hage argues that tolerance is actually on the same continuum as racist exclusion, and that tolerance and intolerance are always closely linked.[7] His main point is that different individuals have different levels of tolerance, but everyone is somewhere on the continuum. All of us still tolerate to a greater or lesser extent, it is just that the more overtly racist have a much lower tolerance level. Tolerance necessarily involves an imbalance of power. Thus, those who are tolerated are regarded as clearly inferior to those with the power to do the tolerating, and those who tolerate hold all the power, which they are asked at this particular juncture to avoid exercising. Hage's particular concern about the notion of tolerance is its covert nature. He argues that it "is a strategy aimed at reproducing and disguising relationships of power in society, or being reproduced through

---

5. Ramadan, *Islam, the West*, 264–304.
6. Ramadan, *The Quest for Meaning*, 47.
7. Hage, *White Nation*, 80–97.

that disguise. It is a form of symbolic violence in which a mode of domination is presented as a form of egalitarianism."[8]

The view that tolerance is closely linked to the exercise of power is supported by the assertion that it is only those who have power who are asked to be tolerant. Those who have no power to be tolerant are not themselves asked to be tolerant, Hage suggests. Whilst there is truth in this observation, it must be nuanced by a recognition that one must be careful in defining power to be intolerant: freedom of expression grants otherwise powerless individuals the ability to vocalize their intolerance. They may have little formal power in society, but they do still have the ability to be intolerant. Thus, for example, a school pupil may have little formal power either in her specific educational context or wider society, yet her intolerance of those different to herself may have a significant impact on her class and indeed the whole school.

Tolerance always presupposes control—an object to tolerate, to manage, to have power over. The question is simply over where the limits are set. Ramadan traces the history of tolerance in the West; noting that it was primarily promoted as a virtue to limit or eliminate conflict, especially conflict within the Christian world.[9] (An example of this would be the 1689 British Parliament Act of Toleration that allowed non-Conformist Christians freedom of worship.) He argues that what was once regarded as a virtue has now become outmoded and perpetuates inaccurate assumptions about the presence of Muslims in the UK (especially that their arrival is recent and that they have no stake in society) and precludes the possibility of an equal relationship. Finally he posits that the promotion of tolerance in fact does little to deal with the reality of intolerance towards Muslims.

In his attack on tolerance, Ramadan finds an ally in Luke Bretherton, who suggests there are three conditions necessary for tolerance. First, there must be conduct about which one disapproves, even if only mildly. Second, the disapprover(s), who have the power to act coercively against or interfere with that of which they disapprove, but chose not to. Third, the lack of interference must result from more than acquiescence, indifference, or a balance of power. Thus Bretherton argues that tolerance is effectively the powerful not wanting something to happen, but choosing to let it happen anyway. He argues that hospitality, not tolerance, is an appropriate Christian response to difference, noting that hospitality has been the primary

8. Ibid., 87.
9. Ramadan, *The Quest for Meaning*, 45–8.

Christian response over the years, that it has greater scriptural warrant, and finally, that tolerance is a very inadequate response to difference.[10] Crane also castigates tolerance, describing it as "the attitude that I will not kill you now, but I will as soon as I get a good chance," and arguing that it reflects an understanding derived from medieval toxicology and pharmacology, which marked how much poison a body could tolerate before it succumbed to death.[11] Tolerance is to be welcomed as a first step, a move beyond hatred, but it is no more than that. It is not a peak to ascend, but a foothill from which to climb towards peaceful cooperation and mutual self-understanding.

In a similar vein, Ramadan argues that rather than promote tolerance, the virtue required is that of respect.[12] Respect requires engagement and knowledge of the Other, and thus a move beyond theoretical assumptions about those different to you, to an active relationship with them, as we "free ourselves from the ghetto of our noble, secure mind in order to enter the world of raw, tenacious, and sometimes mad and dangerous emotions."[13] Tolerance is possible in isolation, but respect requires active engagement between real individuals. Ramadan suggests two verses from the Qur'an that support this view.[14] First the statement that "If God had (so) pleased, He would indeed have made you one community, but (He did not do so) in order to test you by what He has given you" (5:48). The context of the statement suggests that although there are different views about the divine nature, the gift of the Qur'an is a means by which believers come to understand the truth about whom God is. Second, Ramadan notes the power of diversity to exercise some control, supported by the statement that "If God had not repelled some of the people by means of others, the earth would indeed have been corrupted" (2:251). Interestingly he does not cite the verse most commonly used in this context, namely:

> People! Surely We created you from a male and a female, and made you different peoples and tribes, so that you may recognize one another. Surely the most honorable among you in the sight of God is the one among you who guards (himself) most. Surely God is knowing, aware. (49:13).

10. Bretherton, *Hospitality as Holiness*, 122–6.
11. Crane, "From Clashing Civilisations," 177.
12. Ramadan, *Western Muslims*, 110.
13. Ramadan, *The Quest*, 41.
14. Ibid., 48.

This verse summarizes the view that diversity is part of the order of creation, intended by God to provide an opportunity for believers to respond with the godly virtue of respect.

Ramadan is persuasive, and I agree that tolerance is not enough. I understand the sentiment of the verse from the Qur'an above, that difference can, and should, be a means to positive engagement. I would, however, also argue that he hears "tolerance" as implying condescension, a point that was made particularly clear to me when I heard him speak publicly on the issue. His rhetoric was powerful as he told the audience, "No one wants to be simply *tolerated* do they? Do you want me to just *tolerate* you?" with an emphatic disdain lying behind every articulation of this word. Contrary to Ramadan's suggestion, I do not think tolerance is always condescending and indeed many people have nothing but the best intentions in promoting tolerance.

Furthermore, when encouraging those who actively dislike each other to begin to move towards more harmonious relationships, tolerance is the best place to start. It is certainly true, nevertheless, that tolerance is a necessary precursor to respect, and simply remaining at a level of passive toleration is insufficient for the harmonious functioning of a multi-racial, multi-religious community. Working to promote respect is a risky and arduous process, but ultimately a much more rewarding one than simply tolerating difference. This requires deliberate attempts to engage, to confront awkward questions, dealing with them honestly and openly, and to seek to understand and be understood. The path there is neither easy nor short, but the goal is one worth the struggle.

## ALIENATION AND ASSIMILATION: TWIN DANGERS TO AVOID

Ramadan is clear that Muslims must move on from a blame culture and a victim mentality, and choose to engage with wider society. As Muslims do this, they must recognize the twin dangers of alienation and assimilation, both of which might be regarded as the natural responses of a minority group within society.[15] He defines assimilation as being a European Muslim without Islam, and alienation as living as a Muslim in Europe but out of Europe. In the case of the former, one looses all sense of Muslim identity, and in the case of the latter, all sense of European citizenship. Ramadan

---

15. Ramadan, *To be a European Muslim*, 179–98.

criticizes those who are alienated as having confused Islamic teaching with "the way of life and customs of desert inhabitants of the 7th century," and those who assimilate or who promote assimilation as misunderstanding the request "live with us" to mean "be like us."[16]

Moreover, rather than advocating integration, Ramadan is in favor of participation. It may seem odd that he is against integration, until one understands how he defines the term. For Ramadan, integration has connotations of provisionality, of a newly arrived person being helped, perhaps condescendingly, to become part of a society about which she knows little, and to which she has little or nothing to contribute. As with the notion of tolerance, the discourse of integration has an inbuilt imbalanced power structure, and therefore marginalizes Muslims in Europe, failing to recognize how long they have been here. Thus he states, "For those who were born in the West or who are citizens, it is no longer a question of 'settlement' or 'integration' but rather of 'participation' and 'contribution.'"[17]

Ramadan's opposition to integration stems from this simple fact that Muslims are not a newly arrived group in the UK. He explains his point clearly:

> So long as one refers to "integration," one nurtures the perception of two entities based on a feeling of "us" versus "them," of a society that "receives" and of citizens who are still a little "of immigrant origin" and who are "received." The all but obsessive discourse about the "integration" of new citizens is an objective impediment to the positive development of a feeling of belonging.[18]

The most powerful aspect of Ramadan's argument in relation to this point concerns the 7/7 bombers, the four men who detonated bombs on three London underground trains and one London bus on July 7th 2005, killing fifty-two civilians. Ramadan argues that as individuals they were very well integrated in British culture, since they were educated, culturally westernized, socialized in pubs, and planned their actions through meetings in gyms. He regards them as having been legally integrated, intellectually integrated, and culturally integrated. What was lacking was psychological integration: these were individuals captive to an adversarial mindset. The question is thus not about integration but participation.[19]

16. Ibid., 184, 188.
17. Ramadan, *What I Believe*, 5–6.
18. Ibid., 68.
19. Ramadan, *The Arab Awakening*, 31.

## What Kind of Friendship?

Ramadan's argument about integration is very powerful, especially since there has been some form of intermittent contact between the UK and Islam for over one thousand years, and Muslims have been continuously present in this country for well over one hundred years.[20] Moreover, it is important to avoid conflating "integration" and "assimilation," since some proponents of integration do, in reality, promote assimilation, with the infamous Tebbit "cricket test" being a case in point.[21] The term integration has a wide variety of meanings, and the understanding Ramadan deplores is probably that which unhelpfully overlaps with assimilation. Modood has developed a helpful distinction between assimilation, an entirely one-way process; integration, a two-way process, but remaining on an individual level; and multiculturalism, where integration is two-way, involves groups as well as individuals, and works differently for different groups.[22]

As Ramadan states, "The question of Islam has nothing to do with immigration as such, and many Muslims are now American or European citizens: Islam is a Western religion in the full sense of the word."[23] Whilst I concur with the observation that many Muslims are American and European citizens, I am less clear as to what it means for Islam to be a "Western religion." If by this Ramadan means a religion practiced by citizens of Western countries, then that is true. But if he means a religion that shares all Western cultural assumptions and norms, then it is not, as Western liberal society would in no way condone the separation of men and women, still the norm in UK mosques, to pick but one example. March notes the tension between Islam and liberal citizenship, suggesting that although a strong case can be made for positive participation in non-Muslim society, it will never be an entirely trouble free relationship.[24] Given their distinctive place within modern British society, the question remains, how then will Muslims live?

## A MIDDLE PATH OF PARTICIPATION

Ramadan advocates Muslims develop a four-fold understanding of their personal identity, and that this becomes the basis on which they engage

20. Gilliat-Ray, *Muslims in Britain*, 3–53.
21. See Sahin, "Islam, Secularity and the Culture of Critical Openness," 9.
22. Modood, *Multiculturalism and Integration*, 4.
23. Ramadan, *Western Muslims*, 147.
24. March, *Islam and Liberal Citizenship*.

with wider society.[25] These four aspects of identity are understood as a series of concentric circles: First, there is one faith, one practice, and one spirituality at the center; second, an understanding of texts and context surrounding that; third, a focus on education and transmission; and fourth, action and participation. I will consider each in turn.

## One faith, One Practice, One Spirituality

Muslims belong first and foremost to God, a fact that has an impact on all other relationships. Faith in the unity of the one God, which is embodied in religious praxis, is intensified and reinforced through one's spirituality: "spirituality is remembrance—recollection and the intimate energy involved in the struggle against the natural human tendency to forget God, the meaning of life and the other world."[26] The aim is thus to always be living out of a conscious recognition of the presence of God, something which Christians also aspire towards. The precise shape of this recognition will differ, but centering oneself on a personal relationship with God is central to both Christianity and Islam.

## An Understanding of Texts and the Context

Ramadan is clear that for Muslims there is no true faith without understanding both their religious sources (the Qur'an and the *Sunnah*) and also the context in which they live. Muslims cannot remain cut off from society (hence avoiding alienation), nor cut off from the foundations of their faith (hence avoiding assimilation). Instead, there must be a constant movement back and forth between text and context, with the central aim of living harmoniously. Hence there is a need for constant intellectual effort:

> To be Muslim entails struggling to increase one's abilities, seeking tirelessly to know more, to the extent that one might say in the light of the Islamic sources that, when it comes to the cultural dimension, "To be Muslim is to learn." The Prophet said, "Seeking knowledge is an obligation for every Muslim man and woman."[27]

---

25. Ramadan, *To be a European Muslim*, 190–6; *Western Muslims*, 77–85.
26. Ramadan, *Western Muslims*, 79.
27. Ibid., 80.

There is a lot of value in this, although Christianity does not necessarily place such an automatic emphasis on learning in an intellectual sense. But perhaps Ramadan is heading towards the idea of knowing how to live out the story of God's interaction with humanity. N. T. Wright has popularized the idea of Christians, both as individuals and groups, playing their part in the unfinished story of the people of God.[28] Part of this process is translating the language of the world around us into the language of the kingdom of God, a point to which I will return. To give an example from my own profession of Christian minister, Eugene Peterson has critiqued the notion of "success" in terms of numbers attending church, offering in its place a model of "faithfulness" to a calling.[29] The Biblical prophet Jeremiah is one example of someone who saw little immediate success, but was nevertheless faithful to his calling. Thus Peterson translates the concept of success to make it intelligible to someone who is learning to see the world differently, or to "speak Christian."[30]

Ramadan develops his point, suggesting that Muslims need to learn more in order to be better able to make choices between what is good and what is bad. Choices of necessity involve freedom, as without freedom one is unable to choose. Thus there is a need for understanding that is based on knowledge and choice based on freedom. Muslims should be characterized by "*an active and dynamic intelligence* that needs knowledge, freedom and a sense of responsibility."[31]

## Education and Transmission

When he discusses education and transmission, Ramadan is thinking primarily of the family unit. He suggests that a desire to share one's faith with one's family is integral to Muslim identity, and was commanded by Muhammad from the very inception of Islam. The expectation is that parents will be diligent in communicating faith to their children, enabling their offspring to make intelligent and informed choices about whom they follow.

There is also the wider responsibility of the *shahada* to be witnesses to the truth of Islam. But, perhaps in contrast with Christianity, Ramadan

---

28. Wright, "How Can the Bible be Authoritative?"
29. Peterson, *Five Smooth Stones; Working the Angles; Under the Unpredictable Plant.*
30. Hauerwas, *Learning to Speak Christian.*
31. Ramadan, *Western Muslims*, 81.

argues that the "responsibility ends there, for the idea of converting people is alien to Islam: to pass on the message is to call and invite people to a real knowledge of the presence of God and a true understanding of his teachings."[32] He suggests that God, not human beings, brings about conversion.

It is difficult to be certain how this relates to Christianity. There are clear scriptural commands regarding the upbringing of children, such as Proverbs 22:6; Ephesians 6:4, or Colossians 3:21, and most Christian parents would expect to encourage their children to also become Christians, although without coercion or undue pressure. Similarly, Christians understand conversion to be primarily the work of the Holy Spirit, and so arguably do not regard it as something human beings do themselves. Fundamentally, it depends on how the term "witness" is understood. If it includes an active testimony, through words and actions, to the truth of the Christian faith, then I completely share Ramadan's perspective. If, however, it is more passive, and will only respond to direct questioning, without any desire for active engagement, then our understandings differ.

## Action and Participation

Ramadan argues that Muslims must always act according to the teachings of Islam, regardless of their personal circumstances or situation. He is clear that Islam does not commend or command withdrawal from society in order to get closer to God: there is no tradition of the hermit within Islam. A Muslim demonstrates his faith by how he treats other people, and so must be an active member of the society in which he lives.

For British Muslims, there is an expectation that they will develop a method of remaining faithful to these dimensions of their identity whilst also being active in their present society. Ramadan summarizes his point in this way: "For an individual, to bear the faith has to be translated into action that is consistent with it."[33]

The use of the verb "translate" is illuminating. The metaphor deserves further consideration. Any Muslim or Christian seeking to be faithful to her own tradition in contemporary society is engaged in a process of translation. A (overly) simple definition of translation is that it is the process of transferring a text from a source to a receptor language in a manner that is

32. Ibid., 81.
33. Ibid., 82.

intelligible to those who speak only the receptor language. Bellos points out that translations are essential for daily life, whether in business, food labels, or the instructions for flat-pack furniture.[34] More fundamentally, "translation helps us to know, to see from a different angle,"[35] to understand the unfamiliar and see the familiar in a new light. There are many different possible ways to translate a text, but they all have a common objective: making the otherwise incomprehensible comprehensible. Translation is not necessarily linguistic. We translate all the time, as a normal part of daily life, as the frequency of phrases such as "like," "you know what I mean," and "for example" in daily conversation show.

Nida has popularized two prominent theories of how Bible translation can be accomplished.[36] The first is formal equivalence, where one attempts to ensure the message in the receptor language should match as closely as possible to the different elements in the source language. This method is often criticized for producing an overly wooden final product, lacking readability, leading Bellos to discuss the "paradox of foreign-soundingness."[37] Nida's preferred alternative is dynamic equivalence translation, which focuses not on word-for-word correspondence, but rather in replicating the relationship between text and readers. Whang gives the following Biblical example:

> The kingdom of heaven is like an original manuscript in a used books store. When a historian found it, she sold all her other books to buy the manuscript. Again, the kingdom of heaven is like a scientist looking for new projects. When he found one theory of great promise, he joyfully gave up all his other projects to focus on it (See Matthew 13:44–46).[38]

Concern over literalist approaches to translation is common. Grossman, like most scholars of translation theory, is skeptical of the more literal approach, citing a favorite cartoon in which "a bewildered translator asks a disgruntled author, 'Do you not be happy with me as the translator of the books of you?'"[39] The faithful and successful translation will "make a text come alive so that it can be internalized, owned and acted upon

---

34. Bellos, *Is That a Fish in Your Ear?*
35. Grossman, *Why Translation Matters*, xi.
36. Nida, *Towards a Science of Translating*.
37. Bellos, *Is That a Fish in Your Ear?* 41–56.
38. Whang, "To Whom is a Translator Responsible?" 53.
39. Grossman, *Why Translation Matters*, 69.

by a new target group"[40] This requires more than literalism or dynamic equivalence of sentence clauses, as context, culture and the translator's own position are also central to the production of any new text. The text is not just dead letters, but a living and enacted word.

We speak different languages, see the world in different ways, and are influenced by our upbringing, our context, and the language we speak. Yet at the same time we have much in common: we share the same types of feelings, emotions, information, understandings, and so forth. Without these two suppositions—that we are the same and different—translation could not exist. Nor could any form of social life. Thus, to translate is to be human. We are all translators. The question is, what translation methodology do we use?

Ramadan seems to adopt much more of a dynamic equivalence than a literalist approach. He argues that "Islam, with its Islamic sources, is *one and unique*; the methodologies for its legal application are *several*, and its concretization in a given time and place is by nature *plural*."[41] In essence, Muslims are expected to not make concessions on the essentials of their faith, but remain faithful while allowing for evolution to their present context.

This is a perspective shared by many Christians. Hauerwas discusses the metaphor of "speaking Christian" at some length, arguing that learning how to live as a Christian means learning how to speak another language, the language of faith.[42] Christians are charged with speaking in a manner that is faithful to scripture, that does not say more than can be said, and that is an authentic witness to the world of the truth of the Christian faith.

In his reflections on Christian ethics, Hays suggests a similar approach. He argues that one can look in the Bible for rules, principles, paradigms, and for a symbolic world, helping us create the perceptual categories necessary for making informed Christian moral choices.[43] Not all of the Bible can, or should, be read in any one of these ways. The question is determining which mode of appeal to apply to a particular passage. The realm of sexual ethics may serve to illustrate the point. The prohibition against adultery of Exodus 20:14 is a clear example of a rule. However, Proverbs 6:32 (But a man who commits adultery lacks judgment; whoever

40. Sullivan, "Catholic Education as Ongoing Translation," 203.
41. Ramadan, *Western Muslims*, 85.
42. Hauerwas, *Learning to Speak Christian*, 84–93.
43. Hays, *The Moral Vision of the New Testament*, 208–9.

does so destroys himself) can be thought of more in terms of setting forth a principle. The episode of David's adultery with Bathsheba and the ensuing damage both to David personally, and also to the Davidic line (with Ammon and Tamar as one example), could be thought of as a paradigm of the impact of adultery on individuals and on the community around them. In a sense, the record of the episode also sets up a symbolic world, since it helps us create the perceptual categories necessary for making informed Christian moral choices in the area of sexual ethics. The material in Proverbs 7 is also relevant here. It may be difficult to categorize the material, since Wisdom's warnings about the impact of the adulteress can be thought of in terms of a paradigm or alternatively as outlining a series of principles as to why adultery should be avoided.

Hays also suggests the following three authorities, in addition to Scripture, that are used in making ethical decisions: tradition, reason, and experience.[44] Each of these are seen as complementary sources of authority, which stand in harmony with the witness of the Bible rather than as counterbalancing or contradictory. Thus tradition will carry many insights as to how the text has been understood over time, providing the witness of history to the moral decisions of the past. Furthermore, reason helps us to understand what would form a sensible and logical moral choice, although as Hays notes, the gospel of the cross frequently confounds reason. Finally, experience confirms the truth of the teaching of Scripture as confessed and lived out in the community.

Hays proposes the following three focal images for the grammar of faith: community, cross, and new creation.[45] His reasons for choosing these three images are as follows: community because, "The church is a countercultural community of discipleship, and this community is the primary addressee of God's imperatives." Ethics is a communal, not an individual, activity. This is true of all areas of ethical life, since even decisions of sexual ethics, which may appear to be intensely personal, are also ones that affect the wider community.

The cross is key because Jesus' death on a cross is the paradigm for faithfulness to God in this world. In terms of ethics it provides us with the supreme example of self-giving love for us to imitate. Furthermore, the Resurrection, which is implied by the cross, reminds of the super-natural power that is God's and not ours. As Hays also notes, the cross is not just an

---

44. Hays, *Moral Vision*, 209–11.

45. Ibid., 193–205.

individual call, but one which calls the whole community to follow Jesus' way of suffering, where those with power and privilege surrender it for the sake of the weak.

Finally, the new creation embodies the power of the Resurrection and of the Christian future hope in the midst of the not-yet-redeemed world. The hope of the eschatological consummation of the new creation is a major factor in Christian ethical decisions, since choices that may not seem logical to one focused solely on the present become more intelligible in the light of the future hope.

Hays further argues that neither love nor liberation provide suitable focal images for the Christian ethical framework. As Hays notes, love is not a central thematic emphasis for a number of New Testament books, including Mark, Acts, Hebrews and Revelation. Furthermore, love is not really an image, but rather an interpretation of the focal image of the cross. Equally, liberation is not present in Matthew, Ephesians, or the Pastorals, and whilst it does provide a more specific image than love, it is one in danger of an immanent, political interpretation: the loss of the eschatological focus would rob the Christian message on a key element.

These three focal images do not exhaust the New Testament picture of ethics, much less the entire Bible's, but they do provide a useful point of departure for the formation of a Christian ethic. This shows us how we can understand the role of the Bible in Christian ethics. Rather than being a textbook that dictates the solutions to the moral and ethical problems we present, it is a narrative from which, through careful study and interpretation, ethical guidance can be sought. The text cannot be read in isolation, and the influence of other sources of authority must be recognized and sought. But the primary place for making ethical decision must be reserved for the Bible.

This, then, is how one learns to "speak Christian," by gaining great familiarity with the sacred text and relating that carefully, through the three focal images of community, cross, and new creation, with the application of reason, in the light of tradition and experience. Ramadan has developed a similar approach to Muslim social engagement, and in the remainder of this book I will examine specific examples of his approach and contrast them with those advocated by a range of Christian scholars, as representative voices who are aiding me as I read Ramadan.

## WHAT KIND OF FRIENDSHIP?

Christians must not isolate themselves from the world, but live in the world without becoming indistinguishable from those who surround us. The twin dangers of alienation and assimilation are equally real to Christians, although we may not recognize them as such. There is much in Ramadan's middle path of participation which, if appropriated within a Christian framework, would be of great value to a Christian disciple learning how to "speak Christian."

# 5

# Ethics and Medical Science

AT THE HEART OF Ramadan's discussion of issues relating to medical ethics is a conviction that the main aim of any medical intervention is to protect the life, dignity, and welfare of humanity by protecting conscience, personal stability, integrity, and health.[1] He illustrates this with reference to the Qur'anic self-description as providing "guidance and healing for those who believe" (41:44). The discussion about health and medical ethics is thus not solely about the physical body, but about the whole person, and spiritual health is of supreme importance. Ramadan explains:

> The Revelation is a remedy and it calls on believing consciences to strive with all their might—to undertake an intimate *jihad* of the inner being (*jihad an-nafs*)—to preserve their inner health and reach higher well-being.[2]

This means that human beings are first of all responsible to God for their spiritual state, but that secondly they are also responsible for their physical state. In a *hadith* reported by al-Bukhari, Muhammad is reported to have told his audience that their bodies had rights over them, indicating an expectation that Muslims would care for their physical bodies. This is not just an individual, but also a corporate responsibility, mandating not just a focus on personal wellbeing, but also devotion to medical practice.

1. Ramadan, *Radical Reform*, 159.
2. Ibid., 160.

Ramadan advocates studious devotion to medical science, with strenuous efforts being made to cure illness, restore health, and prevent disease spreading. Ramadan also recognizes that much medical science is not necessarily Islamic in nature. He therefore argues not for a distinctive Islamic medicine, but for distinctive Islamic ethics related to medical issues.

Ramadan recognizes that modern medical science has greatly increased the complexity of Islamic medical ethics. The increases in knowledge, and the development of new techniques, treatments, and therapies have all given medical practitioners a great deal of potential power. A simple code of ethics is no longer a sufficient guide to some of the complex decisions that have to be faced. At the same time, scholars of Islamic texts struggle to be able to comment on specific issues because they are becoming increasingly complex. Nevertheless, some efforts must be made at providing guidance for an Islamic medical ethic.

Ramadan tackles three issues in *Radical Reform*: contraception and abortion, euthanasia and organ transplantation, and AIDS. In what follows, I will outline his explanation of the Islamic view before presenting some Christian responses to those views. These are all complex moral issues that have been vigorously debated in both the Muslim and Christian worlds, so what follows will of necessity be a simplification of complex debates. I have engaged in it primarily as a learning process; the comparison between views is, as in the rest of the book, an exercise in challenging my own views, not in scoring points against someone else's.

## CONTRACEPTION AND ABORTION

Ramadan's discussion of contraception and abortion begins by outlining Muslim views on sexual relations. It should be noted that he only discusses heterosexual relations in this context, and there is no reference to issues of monogamy and polygamy.[3]

He explains that the first goal of sexual relations should be the legitimate means for a woman and a man who are married to each other to have children. Thus the end point of the act of copulation should be procreation, and any attempt to stop this should be forbidden, (*haram*) or at least strongly objected to (*makruh*). Although this second view is the most commonly held Muslim opinion, there are those of the more literalist, *salafi* trend who oppose all contraceptive methods, although the Prophet appears

3. Ibid., 167–73.

to have sanctioned coitus interruptus (*al-'azl*) as permissible, provided the woman consented.

Ramadan further states that sex is not just for procreation, but also for pleasure, making reference to a famous *hadith*, reported by both Bukhari and Muslim, in which the Prophet associated lawful sexual intercourse with a pious act, with charity (*sadaqah*), explaining, "In your sexual intercourse with your wives, there is an act of charity." This association of desire and pleasure with spiritual and religious recognition was at first a surprise to his companions, who asked whether fulfillment of sexual desire is something that God rewarded. Muhammad answered: "Tell me, if one of you had had unlawful intercourse, would he not have committed a sin? This is why when he has lawful intercourse he is rewarded for it."

This means that procreation and contraception are not the only issues where sexual relations are concerned. Ramadan suggests that the higher goals of human life are also relevant. Individuals are expected to achieve their wider desires, to enjoy balance and stability in their personal lives, as well as psychological and physical health. Moreover, the welfare of the spouse and wider family are also relevant considerations. This means that family planning in poorer societies has not always been received unfavorably by most Muslim religious authorities because of considerations of social development, children's education, and family welfare. Where there has been opposition, Ramadan suggests that it was more to the colonialist attitudes of "the rich West compelling the South's poor to have fewer children while refusing to be critical of the dominant economic order that maintains indecent privileges and prevents a fair sharing of wealth."[4] Contraception is thus permissible in many circumstances, and sexual relations between a married man and woman is something to be celebrated and enjoyed.

Ramadan suggests that abortion is regarded as an entirely separate issue, on which there are two main stances within Islam. The first regards abortion as disposal of a human being's life, and is therefore forbidden unless the mother's life is at risk. A Qur'anic injunction is taken as applying to the fetus as much as to any child: "Do not kill your children for fear of poverty. We will provide for them and for you. Surely their killing is a great sin" (17:31). On the basis of this verse, abortion is therefore generally regarded as forbidden (*haram*) or perhaps simply objectionable (*mukruh*).

The difference between whether it is viewed as forbidden or objectionable rests, in the main, on conclusions to a more technical debate over

---

4. Ibid., 170.

when the soul or spirit is sent into the embryo, so that the flesh is transformed into a living human being. The discussion centers on interpretation of a *hadith* of Bukhari and Muslim, which notes:

> The conception of each one of you in his mother's womb is accomplished in forty days, then he becomes a clinging clot (*'alaqah*) for the same time, then a lump of flesh (*mudghah*) for the same time. Then an angel is sent to blow life spirit (*ar-rûh*) into him.

Ramadan explains that this, and other similar *hadith*, have led a minority of scholars to suggest that abortion is permitted for the first one-hundred and twenty days (seventeen weeks). They argue that since the soul is absent during this time, the embryo is not yet a human being. No one argues for abortion beyond this date, and there is controversy even about this date and what conditions permit it. Ramadan suggests that individual circumstances should always be taken into account, and so a decision made on a case-by-case basis within these broad parameters. He notes that abortion has been permitted after rape, when prenatal tests revealed irreversible physical or mental deficiencies, and in cases of involuntary or accidental pregnancies, where the family situation or social context would prevent the family's and/or the child's flourishing. In concluding his discussion, he recognizes that some scholars have always argued it is primarily the woman's decision, and she could resort to abortion without the husband's consent. The majority Muslim view is that abortion should generally be avoided, although Steve Connor, writing in the *Independent* newspaper in 2014, argued that there is evidence of certain ethnic groups in the UK, especially those from the Indian subcontinent, practicing gender selective abortion.[5] This practice may not be motivated by Islam, but it is common amongst certain Muslim groups, and presents a particular challenge to the British Muslim population.

## A Christian View

Building on my discussion of Richard Hays' work in a previous chapter, I will use his discussion of abortion as a representative Christian view.[6] It is not the only Christian position, any more than Ramadan's is the only Muslim one. Hays begins his discussion of a Christian ethical view on the

5. Connor, *The Lost Girls*.
6. Hays, *Moral Vision*, 444–61.

topic of abortion by reviewing texts that may be relevant to the discussion. He starts with the Decalogue, and suggests that although Exodus 20:13 and Deuteronomy 5:17 both state, "You shall not murder," there is nothing in the Decalogue, or indeed the Torah, that says abortion can be categorically defined as murder. The one text that has any relevance is Exodus 21:22–5, which discusses compensation following the injury to a pregnant woman, including the death of an unborn child. However, as Hays states, this provision does not tackle intentional abortion, but property law, dealing with unintentional injury. (The Septuagint of this text complicates the issue, but since the Hebrew (Masoretic) text is regarded by the Protestant Church as the Canonical version, I will not include that discussion here).

Both Psalm 139:13–6 and Jeremiah 1:5 proclaim God's divine foreknowledge and care—the former text makes poetic claims about how God is active in the formation of unborn life in the womb. But in Hays' view, this is poetry, not a scientific or propositional statement, and has no direct bearing on the debate about abortion. Similarly, the reference in Luke 1:44 to the child in Elizabeth's womb (John the Baptist) leaping for joy as Mary greets her is a Christological point, not a scientific claim about the personhood of the fetus. Therefore, in Hays' view, the most that can be claimed from Biblical texts is that God providentially cares for all life, even before birth or conception. Not all Christians would share this view, and some would use the texts cited in a manner similar to the Islamic use of the *hadith* referred to above.

Hays develops his argument relating to abortion primarily through reference Scripture, tradition, and reason. Turning first to the symbolic world of the New Testament, he suggests it portrays God as the creator and author of life. Thus, he notes that within a mother's womb, God is at work, and therefore argues that we are God's creatures to whom he has delegated the task of stewarding the life he alone creates. Therefore, "To terminate a pregnancy is not only to commit an act of violence, but also to assume responsibility for destroying a work of God."[7] This view makes no decision as to whether the fetus is a person or not, and allows for the possibility of circumstances in which it might be permissible to terminate a pregnancy. However, the burden of proof lies heavily upon any decision to undertake such an extreme action, and permission could not be lightly or swiftly assumed. Hays uses three analogies from the New Testament to support this argument.

7. Ibid., 450.

First, the Good Samaritan (Luke 10:25–37): the call to become neighbors to those who are helpless, which includes both the fetus and a mother in a crisis pregnancy. Legalistic questions about the personhood of the fetus are on a part with the "limiting self-justifying question that the lawyer asked."[8] If we define the fetus as a non-person, and therefore not worth saving, we are going against the spirit of the parable, which calls us to widen our vision and be merciful to all.

Second, the Jerusalem Community (Acts 4:32–5), which suggests the community should assume responsibility for caring for the needy. This means a mother should not be forced to choose abortion solely on economic grounds: the church should assume responsibility to provide for both mother and child. Hays argues that "Surely the liberal Protestant church's advocacy of abortions for poor women who cannot afford to raise children is a tragic symbol that the church has lost its vision for communal sharing and consequently acquiesced to the power of death."[9] Moreover, he adds, Christian fathers should be subject to the discipline of the community, and expected to provide for their children, planned or otherwise.

Third, the imitation of Christ (Romans 15:1–7; 1 Corinthians 11:1; Galatians 6:2; Philippians 2:1–13). The community of believers is called to forego their own freedom in order to serve others, especially the weak. These exhortations are addressed to a community, not individuals. While only the mother can undergo pregnancy and labor, the wider challenge of raising a child can, and should, be a communal responsibility.

Hays argues strongly that although it does not make any explicit statements, Scripture supports a case against abortion. In the case of reason, the situation is more complex. Hays outlines six commonly used lines of reasoning that the New Testament excludes. First, the notion of rights is excluded, because Scripture does not speak of a "right to life," but rather of life as a gift from God, and does not give us the right to control our bodies, which are given by God to whom we are accountable for their care. Second, the right to privacy is excluded, as Christians are expected to live as people together in community. Third, the "sacredness of life" is a non-argument, because as God's creatures we have no sovereignty over life. Fourth, questions over when life begins are inappropriate as they are unanswerable from either a scientific or a biblical perspective. Fifth, the argument that "unwanted" children should not be born slips too easily into advocating

8. Ibid., 451.
9. Ibid., 452.

infanticide among the poor. Sixth, the hypothetical "what if Mary decided to abort Jesus" and the counter "what if Hitler's mother decided to abort him" are not New Testament reasoning, which asks not the consequentialist question, "What happens if I do X?" but "What is the will of God?"

Finally, Hays suggests experience cannot tell us anything because claim and counter-claim prove so inconclusive. His overall conclusion is that the norm should therefore be against abortion. But what of the exceptions? Hays suggests that in the case of pregnancy as a result of rape or risk to the life of the mother, then abortion is certainly justifiable. In the case of potential serious illness of the child, then the ideal presented by the texts is that this should be a decision of the whole church, who have a duty incumbent upon them to care as a community for the child. The reality is, however, that most local fellowships are not of this caliber, and so the decision, and burden, remains solely that of the parent(s). Returning to his focal images of community, cross and new creation, he suggests how they can be applied in the case of a church caring for both a pregnant teenager and her baby. Community: the congregation's assumption of responsibility for the pregnant teenager. Cross: the girl endures the pain of pregnancy; those who offer to care for girl and her baby endure the pain of providing that care. New creation: the child is baptized and receives the promise of new life.

Although some Christians would dispute aspects of Hays' case, I find it a convincing presentation of a representative Christian view on the topic of abortion. His conclusions are not that dissimilar from Ramadan's. What is striking is the differences in how sacred texts are used to reach that point. Hay's approach is more analogical to Ramadan's more direct approach. This difference is not as strongly present in the discussion of euthanasia, to which I now turn.

## EUTHANASIA AND ORGAN TRANSPLANTATION

Ramadan begins his treatment of euthanasia[10] by re-stating his view of the fundamental premise of Islamic medical ethics, namely that in the light of the requirements of the Islamic conception of life and death *(ad-din)*, every effort should be made to protect life and personal integrity and dignity, while also striving to preserve conscience, autonomy, balance, development, and welfare as far as possible. He considers four types of euthanasia:

10. Ramadan, *Radical Reform*, 173–9.

direct active, indirect active, direct passive, and indirect passive, noting the different levels of complexity in establishing an Islamic view on each.

## Direct Active Euthanasia

Assisted suicide or direct active euthanasia, which consists in giving medication with the intention to cause death to patients who may or may not be at the end of their lives, is strictly forbidden on the basis of the Qur'anic prohibition of suicide. The relevant texts state:

> Do not kill the person whom God has forbidden (to be killed), expect by right [that is for just cause] (17:33)
>
> Do not kill one another. Surely God is compassionate with you (4:29).

(Note that Droge's translation, used in this volume has "Do not kill one another" in the main text and a footnote indicating the more literal translation, "Do not kill yourselves," which is more relevant for Ramadan's argument).

Therefore, although judicial execution and military conflict are permissible, suicide in any form is not. Where there is intense physical suffering, this must be alleviated as far as possible, as suffering is not thought of as intrinsically or spiritually saving, although the Prophet did note that less intense forms of illness and suffering can cause human beings to return to God with patience and trust. Thus, in a *hadith* reported by Muslim, the Prophet said, "The Muslim's situation is most surprising: all that happens to him is good for him; if some good befalls him, he thanks God and that is good for him, and if some evil [illness, pain] befalls him, he bears it patiently and that is good for him."

## Indirect Active Euthanasia

The question of pain relief raises the issue of indirect active euthanasia, where end-of-life patients, who are suffering greatly, are treated. For example a terminally ill patient, whom doctors do not expect to recover, will be given morphine for pain relief. But that morphine can indirectly accelerate the process leading to death. This type of situation has been declared lawful, because the intention is not to take life, but to reduce pain, considering the patient's welfare as death approaches.

## Direct and Indirect Passive Euthanasia

The final set of issues are related to passive euthanasia. The issue here is whether people are always morally obliged to seek medical treatment. Ramadan suggests that the majority Islamic view is that it is recommended (*mustahab*) but not compulsory to seek treatment, although he does note that a minority of scholars argue that it is obligatory to seek treatment.

The majority opinion, that treatment is recommended but not compulsory, means that passive euthanasia is also permitted. Thus a patient is able to cease taking medication or allow for life-support machinery to be turned off. Individual patients, in consultation with their family and the advice and support of medical staff, are free to make these decisions. The aim is to protect dignity and welfare in the light of the irreversible character of the disease. There is therefore a duty incumbent upon wider society generally, and of hospitals and doctors in particular, to provide adequate support for patients in order to enable them to make such decisions and to face death with as much dignity and comfort as possible.

Ramadan raises a concern about the power of machinery, and "technicist ethics" which loose touch with wider social issues. He uses the example of organ donation to illustrate the complexity of the issues, in particular of determining time of death, the permissibility of donating organs (other than the genitals) voluntarily, but the prohibition of any trade in organs under any circumstances. His main concern is that the principle of human dignity and the notion of the human as a whole person is lost to a technocratic pursuit of medical science.

## Christian Views

I will examine two Christian responses to the questions of euthanasia: Nigel Biggar's, which opposes it under any circumstances, and Paul Badham's, which allows for it in some very limited circumstances.

### Nigel Biggar: Aiming to Kill

Biggar's seminal text, *Aiming to Kill*, engages in a careful analysis of a range of views on the question of euthanasia. Biggar's own views are set out clearly in the conclusion. In summary, primarily out of concern that any permission of euthanasia would inexorably lead to a "slippery slope" in which could descend into eugenics, Biggar opposes any relaxation of laws that prohibit euthanasia and assisted suicide. He states, "The special value of the lives of human individuals is best understood in terms of their being dignified by the opportunity and obligation to respond to a call of God to play an inimitable part in the maintaining and promotion of the welfare of the world."[11]

Biggar distinguishes between different types of human life, notably biological and biographical. He suggests that biographical human life is sacred and should not be damaged or destroyed. He recognizes that it is not always possible to realize this ideal, noting that proportionate defense or the pursuit of some good may necessitate the taking of life. In this circumstance, provided one accepts rather than intends (wants) to take life, and provided this acceptance is characterized by a reluctance that is genuine and therefore active, then it is permissible to take life. This can be extended to certain medical situations, but the problem comes in defining which cases are eligible and which are not.

He further argues that protection of the innocent against life-threatening manipulation and abuse is a stricter duty than relief of suffering, and that therefore it is more important to have strict laws forbidding any form of euthanasia than to allow for some types of euthanasia (perhaps direct or indirect passive euthanasia). Having said that, Biggar is not against pain relief for those in extreme pain, including sedation. Equally, he is happy with a terminally ill patient refusing treatment because "He would rather expend his limited energy on living as well and responsibly as possible than on striving to fend off death."[12] Finally, Biggar notes that the most awkward type of case is that of a patient in a persistent vegetative state, but his concerns about a slippery slope mean he maintains opposition to euthanasia in these circumstances. He defends this view with the observation that PVS patients are very small in number, and so their situation is by no means normative.

Biggar's views are thus quite close to Ramadan's. Biggar's acceptance of a terminally ill patient refusing treatment is comparable to Ramadan's acceptance of active and passive indirect euthanasia. The difference may be that Biggar would not define this choice using that terminology. Similarly

11. Biggar, *Aiming to Kill*, 166.
12. Ibid., 168–9.

Biggar's acceptance of pain relief for the terminally ill is probably in the same area as Ramadan's acceptance of passive direct euthanasia. For both, the relief of pain must be the sole motivation and reason for the action. Hastened death may be an outcome, but it cannot be an aim for it to be an action that Ramadan and Biggar could condone, as both are opposed to an active decision by any individual to end his or her own life.

## Paul Badham: Is there a Christian Case for Assisted Dying?

In contrast to Biggar, Badham asks *Is there a Christian case for Assisted Dying?* His book argues in favor of legalized assisted dying for those suffering unbearably in the final stages of terminal illness—a view he contends is supported by many Christians. His discussion is only of this situation, of someone who is competent to make their own decisions and who is suffering unbearably in terminal illness, who repeatedly and explicitly requests assistance to die. He suggests this situation is becoming increasingly common because of increasing longevity, the cost of care homes, and the increasing prevalence of Alzheimer's and dementia amongst the elderly. He also notes that the long, slow death of the elderly is another factor, as is the growth in personal autonomy.

In Badham's view, obedience to the Golden Rule (loving neighbor as self), means accepting assisted dying. His case is, in part, made on the basis of personal experience: having watched his parents and grandparents die, he believes that it was unloving and unchristian that they were unable to opt for a form of voluntary euthanasia. He also suggests that anyone who loves God with heart, soul, and mind would not view death as the ultimate disaster. Rather, death should be regarded as "the gateway to eternal life with God. At death we commit ourselves into the loving hands of God." Badham reinforces this point by telling the story of how, when Cardinal Basil Hume was diagnosed with terminal cancer, he rang the Abbot of Ampleforth, Timothy Wright, to tell him. The Abbot's response was "Congratulations! That's brilliant news. I wish I was coming with you!"[13]

Thus in Badham's view, Christians now cling on to life, rather than embracing the resurrection hope with such strength that death is nothing. He adds that, "When people's sufferings are so great that they make repeated requests to die, it seems a denial of that loving compassion, which is supposed to be the hallmark of Christianity, to refuse to allow their requests

13. Badham, *Is there a Christian case?* 119.

to be granted. If we truly love our neighbor as ourselves how can we deny them the death we would wish for ourselves in such a condition?"[14]

His argument has two further strands. First, he suggests that evidence from both the Netherlands and Oregon (where assisted dying is legal) show that there is no slippery slope, but that on the contrary, the result was greatly increased confidence and trust in the medical profession. Second, he claims that assisted dying could restore the possibility of a Christian deathbed: "One could imagine a situation where a Christian could say goodbye to family and friends, a Holy Communion service could be celebrated at the believer's bedside, and he or she could be given the last rites in preparation for the journey through death to the life immortal."[15]

Badham's case is, in essence, that a Christian can choose to die, and that honoring and assisting that choice is an expression of Christian love and compassion. In this he stands in direct contrast with both Biggar and Ramadan.

## Is there a Christian View on Euthanasia?

These two representative views demonstrate that, as in Islam, there is not a single, monolithic Christian view on the topic of euthanasia. I have not outlined all of the detail of either Badham's or Biggar's reasoning, and it would take me beyond the focus of my discussion to engage with both of their views in great detail. My personal view is closer to Biggar's than Badham's. In particular I find Badham's use of the prevalence of Alzheimer's and dementia amongst the elderly as part of a case for allowing those in full control of their mental faculties to choose to end their own lives a somewhat disingenuous argument. I personally warm more to Giles Fraser's comments that, were he to start contemplating suicide, he hopes his children would bully him out of it.[16] Moreover, I concur with Hauerwas in his argument that life is a gift from God.[17] I can choose to reject that gift, which is a choice to suicide. But in choosing to reject the gift, I also choose to reject the giver, God, who is integral to the gift itself, as human beings were created to achieve fullness of life in relationship with their creator. Therefore, I do not see how an individual can argue that assertion of their

14. Ibid., 121.
15. Ibid., 123.
16. Fraser, *If Christianity is a romance.*
17. Hauerwas, *The Hauerwas Reader*, 585–6.

## Ethics and Medical Science

own will to die, against that of God's that they live, is a loving, compassionate Christian action. The same could be said of assisting an individual in their choice to die. I also concur with Hauerwas that we cannot advocate euthanasia because of a lack of skill or resource to be with, or care for, the dying; that is not killing in the name of mercy, but in the name of failure to care, and that there is nothing wrong with being a burden; bearing other's burdens fulfills the law of Christ, and provides an opportunity to celebrate the life of others.[18] My question about Badham's case is that, although it is emotive and powerful, is whether it is genuinely Christian in it's foundational assumptions, which appear to me to be as much about personal autonomy as about Christian discipleship. Christians can face death without fear and can die in a Christian fashion, filled with resurrection hope, without choosing the exact moment of their death for themselves.

This brief discussion illustrates the fact that there is no single Christian view on euthanasia. Taking the two representative views, if Badham's is accepted as a possible Christian view, then it is markedly different from the Islamic one set out by Ramadan. If Biggar's is seen as the more authentically Christian, then there are greater similarities with the Islamic view, and the process of reasoning is also similar.

### AIDS

Although Ramadan's third area of focus is on the complex moral issues related to the treatment of AIDS,[19] his real concern is on the ethics of treating those whose lifestyle does not conform to Islamic morality. He notes that Islam prohibits homosexuality, expects heterosexual intercourse to remain within marriage, and assumes faithfulness and abstinence to be practiced. This has led to some uncertainties about treating patients suffering from AIDS. In the face of such uncertainty, Ramadan returns to the fundamental premise of Islamic medical ethics that, regardless of religion, race, gender, and moral behavior, medical professionals should not pass judgment, but provide treatment without discrimination or prejudice. Moral principles are relevant for education and preventative work, but not for treatment.

This is a view that Christian medical practitioners would share, probably for similar reasons: human beings are God's creatures, and must be cared for as a part of our stewardship of God's creation and in response to

---

18. Ibid., 591–3.
19. Ramadan, *Radical Reform*, 179–82.

his love and care for each one of us. As Hauerwas argues, the relationship between medicine and Christianity is complex, but at the heart of all medical practice is being present to those in pain, and an attempt to relieve that pain. Christianity provides "a resource of habits and practices necessary to sustain the care of those in pain over the long haul" and so is an invaluable resource for all medical practitioners.[20]

## WHAT KIND OF FRIENDSHIP?

There will be ongoing debates and discussions about medical ethical issues—rulings cannot remain static and fixed, as medical science is advancing all the time. Recent debates over issues such as so-called "three parent babies" make this clear. But the danger of becoming too abstract, too technical or formal must also be guarded against. Reflection must be rooted in reality, and take into account wider considerations of justice and societal wellbeing. Both Christianity and Islam have much to contribute to current medical practice, and should work together to secure moral medicine.

---

20. Hauerwas, *The Hauerwas Reader*, 553.

# 6

# Culture and the Arts

RAMADAN'S OPENING DISCUSSION IN the chapter on culture and the arts in *Radical Reform*[1] is about the relationship between religion and culture. He recognizes that religion is always born and interpreted within a given culture, but at the same time wants to make a clear distinction between the two. He states that "Religion cannot find expression without culture but not all of religion can be reduced to culture."[2] This is an especially complex problem within Islam, where the more conservative interpretations of the faith tend to conflate religious expression with seventh-century Arabic culture. Ramadan is very aware of that danger, commenting on the tendency amongst literalist *salafi* interpretations of Islam to engage in essentially reductionist interpretation whereby religious practice and its cultural interpretation become almost indistinguishable. This occurs primarily because of fundamental methodological presuppositions that Arabic is the true language of Islam and hence the Arab culture of the Arabian peninsular is the true and authentic cultural expression of Islam. Ramadan is critical of such an approach, arguing for the importance of trying "to distinguish religious principles from their cultural garb."[3] He favors this because he is convinced that Islam is a universal religion, which speaks to the diversity of cultures that are present in the world.

1. Ramadan, *Radical Reform*, 183–95.
2. Ibid. 184.
3. Ibid., 184.

## What Kind of Friendship?

Ramadan argues that the problem of establishing the appropriate relationship between religion and culture is not a new one within Islam, since from the early centuries, Muslims living in Africa and Asia had to decide how to relate both to Islam as a religion and to Arabic culture. Creative solutions have long existed in the Islamic world; what is new today is the impact of globalization, and in particular the increasing impact of a single, dominant global culture. The problem in Muslim majority countries is that this dominant, Western culture is seen as imposing itself, and engenders reactions of both attraction and repulsion. This is the common, expected polarity of responses, which should not be understood in binary terms but rather as a continuum between complete rejection and complete assimilation.

The *salafist* literalist trend and the traditionalist stance of some of the *tablighi* movements can be understood as exemplifying the reaction of complete rejection. They respond to perception of imposition of a single, alien, Western universal culture by advocating adoption of a different single universal culture, which aims to replicate all aspects of seventh-century Arabian custom and practice, aiming to live, dress, and interact in a fashion that imitates what the presumed behavior of the inhabitants of Mecca and Medina, on the basis of the texts as they have been received. This is a simple, perhaps oversimplified, solution to a complex and painful experience, and one that Ramadan rejects.

Ramadan's fundamental objection to this solution is that it goes against the teaching of the Qur'an and the practice of the Prophet. Regarding the latter, he notes that Muhammad welcomed the ideas and practices suggested by his companions from different backgrounds and cultures and that he himself experienced exile from the familiar culture of Mecca to the alien environment of Medina. This stance is supported by an often-cited *ayat*:

> And We have sent down to you the Book with the truth, confirming what was with him of the Book and as a preserver of it. So judge between them by what God has sent down, and do not follow their (vain) desires (away) from what has come to you of the truth. For each of you We have made a pathway and an open road. If God had (so) pleased, He would indeed have made you one

community, but (He did not do so) in order to test you by what He has given you. So race (toward doing) good deeds. (5:48).

The Qur'anic understanding is therefore that diversity is a divine gift and test, a means of confirming the truth of the revelation of the Qur'an and of challenging believers to demonstrate their faith in Allah by how they treat others. A particularly important example in this discussion is the Prophet's treatment of *al-Ansar* (the helpers), the people of Medina who became Muslim. They adopted the religion that Muhammad taught, but did not abandon their own cultural practices, including a taste for art and singing, as well as the role of women in society.

Ramadan discusses this experience in greater detail in his account of Muhammad's life.[4] There he describes the exile from Mecca to Medina as a trial of trust, a test of faith in God to see how far believers are prepared to go, and how much they are prepared to give. It also became a means of distinguishing faith and culture, since "Medina meant new customs, new types of social relationships, a wholly different role for women (who were socially far more present than in Mecca), and more complex intertribal relations."[5] Life in Mecca also led to a different attitude to the arts: Ramadan describes an incident where there was a wedding among the *Ansar*, and Muhammad sent two singing maids to the celebrations because he knew they enjoyed singing. It was arguably also a time of liberation, as it allowed the people to become free from oppression, breaking their status as victims, and also spiritual freedom to closer relationship with Allah.

Ramadan argues that the experience of exile in Medina indicates the Prophet was more interested in integrating customs and habits than in assimilating them, although the argument comes in great part from silence, in that the Prophet did not always explicitly state that he accepted different practices, but rather was silent and did not express disapproval. This means that devoted followers of the Prophet in subsequent generations must engage in the same process of working hard to distinguish religious faith from culture. This is not an uncritical process; there is an expectation that while religion and culture are distinguished, there is space for Islam to critique and reform behaviors that are regarded as culturally normal or natural, but nevertheless are ethically questionable.

One example, which Ramadan cites, is of a *hadith* of Bukhari and Muslim, which records an incident where the Prophet kissed his grandson

---

4. Ramadan, *In the Footsteps*, 84–7.
5. Ibid., 85.

in front of a Bedouin. The latter stated that he had ten children, but had never kissed any of them. Muhammad's response was "He who does not spread mercy will not find mercy [with God and men]." This, for Ramadan, is an example of how the Prophet, on the basis of a deep immersion in the spiritual teachings of Islam, was able to challenge established cultural practice.

Ramadan summarizes what he calls the two-fold movement of, on the one hand, "integrating cultural specificities so long as they do not contradict a religion's formal injunctions," whilst also "allowing for critical assessment of the surrounding cultural reference."[6] This process requires viewing both through the lens of religious texts and also through the lens of different cultures, in order to elucidate flaws or deficiencies in one's own culture. This process cannot be prescriptive and top-down but must be a more collaborative effort. An example of this process is the challenge to the practice of female genital mutilation. It is not enough, Ramadan argues, to simply state that FGM is not an Islamic injunction, but is "cultural" and must be stopped. Effort must be made to understand what it represents within the societies where it is practiced, and time taken to progressively change mind-sets and educate as to why this change is necessary.

To simplify somewhat, the struggle is between two modes of interpreting texts. The first is a more literalist reading, which operates by reducing the universal message by prioritizing certain verses or Prophetic traditions without accounting for other Scriptural references or the chronology of their revelation. The second approach is the "cultural" reading, which projects a cultural garb onto the text, allowing or prohibiting practices that are not actually explicitly mentioned in the text.

Ramadan suggests that the diversity of readings that emerge from these two modes of reading texts must be subject to critical and constructive debate about what is truly Islamic. The problem is that everyone remains bound by his or her own context and there has yet to be a realization of this issue within Islamic religious scholarship. Ramadan calls for a rereading to be carried out, a challenge to all those who interpret texts to ensure that their understandings are genuinely about core Islamic beliefs and not about personal cultural presuppositions. His views are supported by those of Hamid Mahmood, whose MA thesis discusses the training of Islamic scholars in UK *dar al-aloom*, noting that teaching is all focused

---

6. Ramadan, *Radical Reform*, 188.

on perpetuating medieval interpretations of texts, with no space given for critical re-reading.[7]

## A Christian Response

I will make three points in response. The first is that this is a debate that has already taken place within (Western, Protestant) Christianity. Anthony Thiselton's work is of particular relevance to the discussion, as he has adapted Gadamer's ideas as expressed in *Truth and Method* in his seminal work *The Two Horizons*, as well as in his subsequent writing. The tension between the horizon of the original text and the horizon of the contemporary audience is one that Christian scholars have been wrestling with for several generations, whilst Ramadan's writing suggests that the Islamic world is only beginning to engage with these issues. I will return to this point subsequently, in the section entitled "Christian hermeneutics" below.

The second point to consider is the relative status of religious texts: the status of the Bible in Christianity is not the same as that of the Qur'an within Islam. The most theologically conservative of Christians are still very comfortable with translated texts in a way that theologically conservative Muslims are not. This means that the relationship between religion and culture is markedly different. Knowledge of first-century CE Mediterranean culture is an important asset in Biblical interpretation, but it does not have the status that knowledge of custom and practice in seventh-century Mecca might have within Islam. The different understandings of text and language, and the different roles translation plays within religious life are crucial for the different ways in which Christianity and Islam engage with the relationship between religion and culture.

The third point flows from this: Christianity has always had a more relaxed approach to art and music than Islam. Indeed they are integral to practice of the Christian faith in many traditions. Some form of music is central to virtually all types of Christian corporate worship, and visual displays (not necessarily icons or paintings or stained glass) are also important in how faith is expressed. I think this difference comes from the Christian doctrine of the incarnation, which assumes that God is intimately involved in human society. God taking human flesh in a particular culture gives value to all cultures in a way that the revelation of the Qur'an in Arabic does not.

7. Mahmood, *The Dars-e Nazimi*.

Ramadan proposes this Qur'anic text is central to a successful project to rediscover Islam as a religion and not simply as an expression of seventh-century Arabian culture: "People! Surely We have created you from a male and a female, and made you different peoples and tribes, so that you may recognize one another. Surely the most honorable among you in the sight of God is the one among you who guards (himself) most. Surely God is knowing, aware" (49:13).

This process must take place in an orderly and respectful fashion: the aim is not simply to challenge or provoke, but to come to the heart of what is genuinely Islamic. It is important to resist both "uniform appropriation of the texts' initial meaning by the original Eastern culture" and also "the homogenization imposed by Western culture."[8] Ramadan's concern is that in resisting the literalist *salafist* trend within Islam, the faith is not swallowed up by Western culture and looses all distinctiveness. Thus he is concerned that an overly simplistic "clash of civilizations" complex might mar the debate, forcing people to make false choices, to fail to understand the complexity of personal identity or the riches of their faith.

Ramadan argues on the basis of an Islamic understanding that in principle anything not explicitly forbidden is in fact permitted, that both literalist Islam and homogenizing Westernism should be resisted, promoting instead a broad cultural diversity, which celebrates and enjoys differences in, for example, styles and tastes of food and drink. The Qur'anic injunction that diversity exists to increase knowledge of the other is also central to developing this view, which enriches personal, inner spirituality as well as the richness of human communities. He summarizes his case as follows: "Concretely, this means remaining faithful to higher principles and ethical objectives, wherever one may be, while developing a curiosity and creativity that make it possible to integrate aesthetic models and artistic expressions from all cultures and backgrounds."[9]

There is no one single, standard Islamic understanding of how to do anything, not even building a mosque, and it is entirely possible to find authentic expressions of Islam which are also true to local cultures. Realizing this vision entails recognizing that there is no such thing as a value-free, neutral public square, and we would be naïve to think otherwise. Religious and cultural symbols "tell of societies' roots and soul," and must

---

8. Ramadan, *Radical Reform*, 193.
9. Ibid., 194.

be respected.[10] Respectful dialogue over time will enable people to develop a means of remaining faithful to the ethical principles of Islam whilst also providing an authentic expression of the culture in which the Muslim lives.

## ENTERTAINMENT CULTURE

Ramadan recognizes the importance of entertainment, but suggests that its primary function should be as a pause, to "give rest to mind, heart and being," before returning to responsibilities regarding life, work, society, justice, and death.[11] This understanding is supported through reference to a *hadith* of Bukhari and Muslim in which the Prophet told one of his companions that it was not good to remain constantly in a permanent spiritual state, remembering God, but that time should be given to devotion and remembrance of God, and time given to rest, distraction, and entertainment. The problem comes when entertainment is no longer a pause or a diversion, but becomes the main or sole activity that someone engages in. Thus when everything has become "dangerously entertaining," it is important to establish an ethics of entertainment in order to determine the proper place of entertainment within one's life.

Ramadan argues that "entertainment is a necessity of life" for people of all ages, and opposes those who would do away with it.[12] But at the same time, he is concerned about balance. Entertainment is a pause, but it must not be a reverse. That is to say, it should not promote values contrary to the higher goals of welfare, balance, and sound development, nor to the general ethics of Islam. Thus, although entertainment should of course be fun, there are serious fundamental ethical questions that must be asked of any particular form of entertainment or play. Ramadan suggests we should question whether the main objective is self-forgetfulness or whether it is an invitation to travel, something that "stirs the heart, mind, and imagination while edifying, soothing and appeasing them with amusements which strive to be human." We should not become slaves addicted to our sensations and emotions, on an endless quest for entertainment and play where all else is forgotten. Instead, we must strive for entertainment that makes us more balanced, freer, more human. In order to achieve this, we must think about the nature of the proposed activities, their time, space, and

10. Ibid., 195.
11. Ibid., 196.
12. Ibid., 196–9.

place. He argues that there is a tendency in Muslim societies to either pack amusement with religious references so that it is no longer recreation or else to reduce all entertainment to childish pursuits, refusing to allow adult Muslims the opportunity to enjoy recreation as Muslim adults.

Ramadan therefore identifies a real need for those who possess the skill and inclination to develop means for adult Muslims, in particular, to enjoy recreation in a manner that is consistent with Muslim ethics. The two pressures that were identified earlier in the chapter are especially relevant here. Ramadan suggests that Muslims are caught between the tendency to forbid everything, which makes life arid or intolerable, and the realities of a carnival of life that alienates them.

My own fieldwork amongst Muslim children in a primary school suggests many younger Muslims are very attracted by the "carnival of life" which Ramadan is concerned will draw them away from an authentic Islamic spirituality. Many of the children I engaged with were keen to enjoy Western pop music and films and only played *nasheeds* (Islamic chants) when their parents came into their rooms.[13] The reality of Ramadan's concerns are demonstrated by the behavior of these children, who did not see the possibility of entertainment that was both genuinely fun and genuinely faithful to Islam.

Ramadan wants people to resist the alienating, standardized global culture, and that requires education and courage, the training of critical minds and good taste, the valuing of imagination and equipping and fostering of activities that encourage it. In an earlier book, Ramadan develops four criteria, which, if met, make music and singing permissible in his view. First, the content of the singing or the type of music must remain in agreement with Islamic ethics and not foster an attitude that contradicts them. Second, and related, the interpretation of the music (by which Ramadan means its mode, moment, and place) must also respect these ethics. Third, this kind of entertainment must not lead people to forget their obligation towards God and fellow human beings. Fourth, it is appropriate for the musician and the audience to measure, in full conscience, the place that this art really takes in their lives. In Ramadan's view, it is a question of establishing a balance of conscience that must be personal and individual.[14] Similarly, when discussing drawing and photography, Ramadan recognizes the concern of Muslims that these practices could lead to idolatry, and so offers guidance.

---

13. Wilson, *Hospitality and Translation*, 154.
14. Ramadan, *To be a European Muslim*, 201–4.

He suggests the intention and content of the drawing photography or film must not contravene Islamic principles or ethics. Furthermore, on a more personal level, it is up to individuals to evaluate their intentions conscientiously and to consider the meaning and place of drawing, photography, and cinema in their own lives in view of their obligations towards God and other human beings.[15] A number of other authorities offer similar guidance. Thus al-Qarawadi notes that "If someone wants to make a picture of an animate being with no intention of competing with Allah as creator or for its glorification or respect, there is no prohibition of doing so; there are numerous sound *ahadith* in this regard."[16] One of the first converts to Islam in the UK, Abdullah Quilliam, re-wrote Christian hymns so that the lyrics were suitable for Muslims to sing.[17]

Conscience also plays an important part: people must remain consciously Muslim even when they are being entertained. The fact that contemporary Islamic thought is unsure of how to do this is a serious problem, because entertainment is vital to proper human flourishing; without it we will simply wither and perish.

## THE ARTS: GOALS AND ETHICS

Islam does have views of the ethics of art, but in Ramadan's view, there is no Islamic justification for the complete exclusion of art. In *Radical Reform* he rejects the view that Islam opposed poetry, painting or music, and refers to the arguments he has made elsewhere (cited above) in support of this position.[18] He suggests that, in the face of the standardization of global culture and its artistic expression, it is all the more important to develop engagement with the artistic world. He opposes the view of the primacy of prohibition (*haram*), reiterating his belief in divine permission giving.

Ramadan recognizes the power of literature, painting, music and movies on the collective imagination, and therefore suggests they are important and must be engaged with. He notes the power of these media and their impact on Western society, suggesting Nietzche, Dostoevsky, Camus, and Sartre as examples of those who have used the arts to influence collective imagination and ethical consciousness. Muslim individuals and societies

---

15. Ibid., 204–6.
16. Al-Qaradawi, *The Lawful and the Prohibited in Islam*, 110.
17. Geaves, *Islam in Victorian Britain*, 84.
18. Ramadan, *Radical Reform*, 199–203.

must therefore ask themselves about the meaning of the arts, the objectives invested within it, and the prospects that it offers to them.

It is not enough to simply add a thin religious veneer, a few Islamic references, a word or two in Arabic, or a touch of spiritual emotion. Ramadan suggests we must reflect fundamentally on the meaning and role of imagination in our lives, how we express our creativity and how we engage with literature, music, and art in general. We must protect the diversity of expressions from the possibility of homogenization and loss.

Faith needs art, and art expresses faith. Moreover, he argues, art asks questions, while faith supplies answers. Ramadan suggests, "It is important for faith to allow the heart a space where it can express with *freedom* and *dignity* its simple, human, painful questions, which may not always be beautiful but are never absolutely ugly."[19] Art thus becomes a means of expressing human identity and understanding, of developing as a whole person and protecting the identity of one's society. Although his argument is aimed primarily at a Muslim audience, there is much for Christians to learn from as well.

Ramadan suggests that in the face of the increasing reach of a globalized, standardized, Western culture, which reaches even the poorest homes in the most remote places, more must be done to establish a rigorous, viable Islamic alternative. His primary concern is that young people throughout the world define themselves primarily in relation to American music and films, and contemporary Islamic thought does not provide any viable alternatives. He does not favor censorship or control, but rather conscience as the guide to developing authentically Islamic artistic expression. His case is that:

> What is at stake is not to produce "Islamic" songs that only speak of such "Islamic" motives as God, the Prophet, respecting parents and norms, and similar things; it is to express through art the feelings and experiences that are part of humankind's hearts and daily lives, with talent and art. I repeat, speaking about childhood, fears, tensions, desires, love, friendship, wounds, separations, hopes, and death in an intimate, natural, universal way *is* "Islamic" and it is not necessary to add specific references linked to a Universe of norms, such as verses, *ahadith*, or Arabic words to give the impression that the work or product has been "Islamized." Such

---

19. Ramadan, *Radical Reform*, 202.

an attitude reveals a deep lack of self-confidence in the forms of culture and art in general.[20]

Ramadan concludes his discussion with a strong call for genuine artistic expression, which remains faithful to the ethics of Islam. The issue is not settling the debate as to what is *haram* and what is *halal* in television, movies, and music. It is about "reconciling art with imagination, music with spirit, literature with the inner-self."[21]

Ramadan raises many complex issues in this chapter, and I will outline two complementary Christian responses to the issues he tackles. First, I will outline some responses to the hermeneutical issues raised at the start of the chapter. In the section that follows, I will examine a particular Christian theology of sport, as an example of Christian reflection on entertainment and play. This is but one example of many possibilities as there are many Christian sub-cultures of different cultures as well as many Christians involved in different cultural expressions.

## CHRISTIAN HERMENEUTICS

In this section, I will briefly examine arguments put forward by three Protestant Christian experts in hermeneutics, outlining strategies for reading texts. These scholars are Anthony Thiselton, Grant Osborne, and Kevin Vanhoozer.

In the introduction to a work that sums up much of his teaching career, Thiselton states that the hermeneutical questions that flow from reading the Bible are quite complex.[22] There are biblical and theological questions; there are philosophical questions about how we understand; there are literary questions about types of texts and processes of reading; there are sociological questions about how vested interests, of class, race, gender, or prior belief influence the reading process; and there are questions about the process of communication, issues of linguistics about how content is communicated to readers or a community. He explains that hermeneutics concerns asking ourselves what we are doing when we read, understand, or apply texts.

---

20. Ibid., 205.
21. Ibid., 206.
22. Thiselton, *Hermeneutics*, 1.

## What Kind of Friendship?

Thiselton suggests three types of insights are gained from the serious study of Biblical hermeneutics.[23] First, texts are read in a new light. This primarily involves letting the text speak for itself, avoiding premature assumptions but also reading with a measure of critical suspicion, recognizing the ease with which one can be deceived by self-interest. Second, the interdisciplinary nature of Biblical hermeneutics has an integrating function, allowing formerly discrete and disjointed areas of study to become a more integrated whole. Third, hermeneutics produces habits of respect for and a more sympathetic understanding of, viewpoints and arguments that previously seemed alien or unacceptable. Hermeneutics is thus an exercise in bridge building.

Reading texts is not a static, but a dynamic process. Thiselton recognizes the importance of beginning with "pre-understanding" (from the German *Vorverständnis*). This is a preliminary understanding of a text, a provisional place from which to build a bridge or begin moving forward to a deeper, more nuanced and rounded understanding. He likens the process to completing a jigsaw: one begins with a general idea of what the final picture looks like, first puts into place a framework, and then fills in the details.

A complementary perspective is provided by Osborne, who views hermeneutics as both a science and an art.[24] It is a science requiring logical, orderly classification of the laws of interpretations. But it is also an art, requiring both imagination and an ability to apply those laws to specific texts. He likens the process of reading to a "hermeneutical spiral," explaining that,

> A spiral is a better metaphor [than that of a hermeneutical circle] because it is not a closed circle but rather an open-ended movement from the horizon of the text to the horizon of the reader. I am not going round and round in a closed circle that can never detect the true meaning but am spiraling nearer and nearer to the text's intended meaning as I refine my hypotheses and allow the text to continue to challenge and correct those alternative interpretations, then to guide my delineation of its significance for my situation today.[25]

---

23. Thiselton, *Hermeneutics*, 5.
24. Osborne, *The Hermeneutical Spiral*, 21–2.
25. Osborne, *The Hermeneutical Spiral*, 22.

## Culture and the Arts

Thiselton is complementary about this metaphor of a hermeneutical spiral, arguing that it has two main strengths.[26] First, it outlines the upward and constructive process of moving from pre-understanding to a deeper understanding, which is constantly checked and reviewed as the reading process develops. Second, it allows for a continual dialogue between pre-understanding and the understanding that flows from a deeper reading, meaning that early assumptions are continuously re-examined for coherence and their relationship to understanding the whole text. The reading of texts is therefore understood very much as an open, not as a closed, process.

Vanhoozer challenges many postmodern approaches to texts. Since Ramadan does not engage with these reading strategies, I will not discuss the detail of his argument here. Instead I will outline some of the points Vanhoozer makes that relate more closely to Ramadan's own preferred reading strategy. First, I will outline the five possible reading strategies Vanhoozer identifies and, second, elucidate in more detail the strategy he adopts, which is similar to the one Ramadan advocates.

Vanhoozer suggests there are five possible modes of reading a text. *Cognitive zealots* claim certain literary knowledge, that there is a single correct interpretation of a text, which can be reached through enough hard work. The problem with this approach is that no one has yet produced a literary work with a single correct interpretation. At the other end of the hermeneutical spectrum are *cognitive atheists*, who exclude the possibility of any single correct interpretation of a text existing. Between them are *critical believers*, who believe in the possibility of a single correct interpretation of a text, but recognize it is difficult to know when it has been reached. These three approaches all embody a form of hermeneutic exclusivism. Vanhoozer also suggests some read texts as *hermeneutical inclusivists*, recognizing there are a finite number of correct interpretations of a given text. Finally, *hermeneutical pluralists* believe that many, perhaps all, readings of a text are equally valid. Vanhoozer himself is probably a *critical believer*, recognizing the possibility of a single correct interpretation of a text, but also knowing he may well not be in full possession of it. Human knowledge remains fallible and provisional, but there is nevertheless the possibility of one day attaining full knowledge.[27]

Vanhoozer's view is, arguably, similar to the critical re-reading which Ramadan advocates. Vanhoozer notes that his views on authorship are

---

26. Thiselton, *Hermeneutics*, 14.
27. Vanhoozer, *Is there a meaning in this text?* 294–5.

integrated with his views about God, suggesting that the traditional picture of both the author as source of meaning of a text, and of God as Supreme Being, assume agency and intelligence standing outside of and controlling language, ensuring words correspond with the world and guaranteeing the reliability and meaning of a text.[28] Ramadan likewise argues for a reading that is faithful to the text but that is also relevant to the culture in which the reader lives. He is advocating a movement that is reflected in Thiselton's *The Two Horizons* where the "horizons" refer to those of the ancient text and of the modern reader. In that book, Thiselton wrestles particularly with the problems of moving from pre-understanding to a deeper understanding, the distance between the historical text and the modern reader, and the need for a sharpened, critical understanding of a text that is nevertheless open to the guidance of the Holy Spirit as the reading is developed. The sophistication of the work of Thiselton, Vanhoozer, and Osborne is not present in the single chapter of Ramadan's work that I have discussed here. Doubtless this is at least partly due to limitations of space. But it probably also reflects the wider reality that Christian discussions of texts are more subject to secular critical academic enquiry than their Muslim counterparts. Opening religious texts to critical scrutiny while remaining committed to reading them as divinely inspired Scripture is, I believe, possible. But it is a difficult balance to keep. Experience in this area is, perhaps, something Christians have to offer in dialogue with Muslims.

## A CHRISTIAN THEOLOGY OF SPORT

One of Ramadan's central concerns in this chapter concerns the place of entertainment in the life of a believer. In what follows I will use one theologian's reflections on sport as an example of a possible Christian response. Although there is not a vast amount of literature on the topic, a few systematic theologians have developed a Christian theology of sport. In what follows, I will outline the persuasive arguments of Lincoln Harvey, as set out in his *Brief Theology of Sport*. He begins by discussing the different attitudes that Christians have had to sport over the centuries. Beginning with the early church, he identifies three phenomena: first, the use of sport by Christians, especially of sporting metaphors to describe the Christian life and for health benefits; second, suspicion and distancing from the sporting performance, especially when associated with pagan religion; and third,

---

28. Ibid., 71.

the prevailing popularity of sport, amongst Christians and non-Christians alike. Harvey suggests the same three phenomena were also present in the medieval period, although suspicion rested now not on athletics, as in a previous era, but on tourneying, both for the associated violence and potential legitimization of adultery. He also finds the three phenomena present amongst the puritans and the subsequent evangelical revivals of the eighteenth and nineteenth centuries. Christians, Harvey concludes, have a mixed relationship with sport, using it for their own ends while also being suspicious of it, and at times distancing themselves from it. But through it all, sport remains unfadingly popular.

Sport, Harvey notes, is a type of play. He defines play as an expression of freedom, noting that no one can be forced to play, but it must always be a free choice. Play is not necessary for survival, but is something we choose to do; people cannot be coerced or forced to play. Play always takes place in guarded time, and often in a guarded space (such as in a playground or sports field). Play, especially organized sport, is bound by rules, which although arbitrary are nevertheless fundamental to the possibility of play. Thus for example, there is no reason why three teams of fifteen could not play in a soccer match, but the rules state it must be two teams of eleven. The rules of a game are arbitrary, but the success of the game is contingent on their being followed. Finally, play, Harvey notes, is superfluous, for nothing. Its aim is simply to be played; it is *autotelic*, having "its own (*auto*) purpose (*telos*), enjoying relative independence from the rest of life."[29] Play, whether spontaneous or regulated, is just play.

Having defined play, Harvey then develops his theology of sport. He begins by discussing the freedom of God in creation; God freely chose to create, he did not do so out of necessity or compulsion. God is therefore distinct from creation, and all that exists does so because of the free gift of his grace. In sum, "We are created freely out of nothing, and remain irreducibly and unavoidably at the mercy of God."[30] This is not a burden or cause for fear, but a release. It should not be grounds for despair; although we were created from nothing, we were created for something, to know and love our creator. Harvey finds parallels with his understanding of play. Creation is arbitrary but purposeful. The precise nature of what God chose to make was decided freely by him, but, having decided, he had a specific purpose in mind—that we would know and love God through the Son,

29. Harvey, *Brief Theology*, 69.
30. Ibid., 81.

Jesus Christ. Thus, Harvey concludes, "When we play—unnecessary but meaningfully—we are living out our deepest identity as unnecessary but meaningful creatures. We chime with our being."[31]

It is on the basis of this understanding of the parallels between creation and play that Harvey builds his theology of sport. Sport has always remained popular, he suggests, because people were created to play (sport). The Church should therefore celebrate all forms of sport that are morally and ethically acceptable. He also argues that sport should not be harnessed for the agenda of the church, but should be left alone, and enjoyed simply as the *autotelic* play it is. Harvey finds similarities between sport and worship: both are activities with their own inner logic, their own intrinsic values, and their own proper ends. Yet it is the ends that distinguish them: sport is primarily about human beings, but worship is about God. It comes down to orientation. Sport is inward focused, but worship looks outwards. When we meet together for corporate worship, we are "travelling together towards the very edges of our being and gazing out beyond ourselves into Life himself (who we find is heading back our way, from every direction)."[32]

## WHAT KIND OF FRIENDSHIP?

My reading of Ramadan on the issue of culture and the arts has led me to conclude there is a significant difference between his approach and that of the representative Christian authors I have engaged with. All of the authors cited have a deep appreciation for culture and the arts, but the basis of their approach differs. The Christian authors engage positively with Western culture and art in a way Western Islam has yet to do so. This may simply be a function of history: as more generations of Muslims live in the West, they may become better equipped for this task. There are some signs that this is the case, of which the popular Muslim lifestyle magazine *emel*[33] is but one example. Perhaps Christians should be showing Muslims how to participate in the cultural and artistic life of their countries in a positive way?

---

31. Ibid., 84.
32. Ibid., 112.
33. www.emel.com

# 7

# Women: Traditions and Liberation

THE TITLE OF THIS chapter, which is taken from that used in *Radical Reform*, reflects Ramadan's concerns in tackling the emotive topic of the position of women within Islam.[1] It is a complex issue, and certainly one that is likely to engender controversy. I am a man discussing another man's views about the place of women within society and a particular religious tradition, and I recognize that some would argue this is an (almost) impossible task to complete fairly. But discussions about the role of women in society cannot be an exclusively female one, and this is a subject that should be discussed. Although I will make every effort to avoid causing offence (as I have done in every chapter), I apologize for any unintended offence caused.

I concur with Ramadan that any discourse about the position of women in society will reveal the collective mind-sets of the conversational protagonists, their fears as well as where they feel confident, their spoken and unspoken assumptions and the foundations of their social world. When the place of women within Islam is discussed, there is a tendency to concentrate on particular problems. Ramadan, however, is keen to move the debate away from what he regards as an endless—and fruitless—cycle of debate around certain hot topics, of which he names dress, polygamy, violence, and inheritance as the four that most commonly occur. This is not out of a desire to belittle or ignore these very real issues, but rather from his recognition that combative claim and counter-claim will not produce

1. Ramadan, *Radical Reform*, 207–32.

fruitful dialogue that leads to any meaningful change. In tackling the issues raised by the status of women in Islam, Ramadan is keen to avoid two pitfalls. The first is an overly close focus on specific texts that speak directly to the issue without recognizing the wider issues of reading the texts in the political and social contexts in which they were written. Essentially, his concern is that overly close focus on a few individual trees means sight of the whole wood may be lost. His second concern is that Western agendas do not drive reform within Islam, either in the sense of attempts at change being made to suit a Western agenda, or in reaction against it. He recognizes that much that is fruitful has come from the "long and intense debates and confrontations in modern societies about the issue of womanhood,"[2] but at the same time, he would rather begin from a close scrutiny of texts and the interactions between early interpreters and their cultural environment, than from a more recent agenda. This is not an attempt to avoid difficult questions. Ramadan is clear that bold questions need to be asked. He is certain that everything is open to scrutiny. But he is also convinced that only a genuinely Islamic agenda is suitable for the process.

Ramadan's discussion focuses initially on the Qur'anic text, and he recognizes that at first only the masculine plural was used to refer to believers, but this was not always so. He cites a key text that mentions men and women separately:

> Surely the submitting men and the submitting women, the believing men and the believing women, the obedient men and the obedient women, the truthful men and the truthful women, the patient men and the patient women, the humble men and the humble women, the charitable men and the charitable women, the fasting men and the fasting women, the men who guard their private parts and the women who guard (them), the men who remember God often and the women who remember (Him)—for them God has prepared forgiveness and a great reward. It is not for a believing man or a believing woman, when God and His messenger have decided a matter, to have the choice in their matter. Whoever disobeys God and His messenger has very clearly gone astray (33:35–6).

The significance of this passage comes in the fact that both men and women are mentioned. The Qur'an does recognize men and women as both created by God (53:45; 75:39; 92:3) but invariably the Qur'an uses the

---

2. Ibid., 209.

masculine pronoun to refer to all believers regardless of gender (although note 4:124; 16:97; 40:40 as exceptions). This inevitably biases understanding in favor of male supremacy, and can lead to patriarchal and misogynistic understandings of texts. Ramadan's point is that this passage is the exception that proves such views to be false: men and women are equal in the sight of God; all are expected to be devout and all are called to account for their lives, regardless of their gender. Bible translators face a similar issue. In one or two places, women are referred to explicitly, such as "suppose a brother or sister" (James 2:15), but often the original refers only to the male (man, brother), and translators have to choose whether to adopt literal or gender inclusive translations.

One of Ramadan's key points is that the message the Prophet Muhammad brought was a radical challenge to the culture of the time, where women were sometimes killed at birth because their fathers were hoping for a son, not a daughter. Thus he states that the "Creator addresses women as being on an equal footing with men, their status as beings and believers the same as men's, and the requirements of worship absolutely identical."[3]

The exile to Medina was crucial in developing the role of women within Islam, as women in that city were more involved and assertive in public life than they were in Mecca. Ramadan suggests that this period in the early formation of Islam was crucial for separating Meccan Arab customs from the religious principles of fledgling Islam. This shift is crucial for understanding the Qur'anic texts and the Prophet's own practice, which developed over time and through his experience in these two very different settings. He argues that although the texts may not initially appear revolutionary when judged by today's standards, once one delves into a more detailed study of the texts, it become apparent that they were far more challenging to the status quo than it may at first appear.

Thus Ramadan argues that women's spiritual quest is recognized as integral to their being, and it is imperative that they achieve a good education. They are recognized as autonomous, with the right to acquire property and goods and manage them by themselves. They have a right to keep their family name when they marry, a right to sexual pleasure, to their own choices regarding marriage, divorce, contraception, and abortion. Ramadan suggests that the views of many Muslim commentators about the role of women in society are influenced more by their cultural presuppositions than by a careful critical reading of sacred texts.

3. Ibid., 210.

## What Kind of Friendship?

In his account of the life of Muhammad, Ramadan argues that Muhammad came primarily to model love and forgiveness to the world.[4] He describes him as a man motivated by justice and the equal treatment of all, regardless of race, gender, or social position. There are a number of *ahadith* that recount how he enabled women to divorce their husbands, something not normal in seventh-century Mecca. Fundamentally, Muhammad "conveyed to women the twofold requirement of spiritual training and asserting a femininity that is not imprisoned in the mirror of men's gaze or alienated within unhealthy relationships of power or seduction."[5] Thus women were expected to play a full and active part in society, but one that was in accordance with the spiritual and ethical requirements of Islam.

Ramadan's central concern relates to the risks of literalist reduction and cultural projection unduly influencing how these texts are read. He spends quite a lot of time discussing these concerns in relation to the issue of the status of women in Islam. It is probably a reflection of his concern to speak to his main target audience, namely Muslims who are sensing the need for some sort of change within Islam in relation to this issue. Certainly, my experience of engaging with Muslims over the past few years is that some younger Muslims, male and female, are questioning the validity of current practices within the overwhelming majority of UK mosques, most notably the fact that provision of space for women to pray is almost always much more inadequate than what is provided for men. Questions are also raised about the possibility of women taking on positions of leadership, both in terms of the role of *Imam*, of leading congregational prayers, and also in governance responsibilities, sitting on the mosque committee and so forth. Outside of religious settings, questions about clothing, career choice, and personal relationships are also quite common.

Part of Ramadan's focus is on restoring the equality of women within society, and so he suggests that leaders within Islam must speak out against those practices that prevent this. These include keeping women illiterate or forbidding them to work, forced marriages, female genital mutilation, denial of divorce, and restraint of domestic violence to name a few of the more pressing issues. It is difficult to be clear as to the extent to which these are serious issues within the United Kingdom at present. My own experience, and the limited research I have been able to access, suggests that there are real issues, and that they are not as widely discussed or challenged as

---

4. Ramadan, *In the Footsteps*, 211–6.
5. Ibid., 213.

they probably should be. Thus, for example, although I have no concrete evidence of whether female genital mutilation took place among communities I have worked amongst, academic research amongst some Somali communities in the UK suggests it is quite probable.[6] Similarly, Ansari details a comparison between Somali and Bangladeshi women in London, which found that the Somalis were more able to attain financial independence from their husbands than the Bangladeshis, whether this was older women working as hospital cleaners or factory workers, or younger women developing their own careers.[7] There are many complex factors involved, and this book is not the place to explore them in more detail. My intention in citing these examples is simply to demonstrate that Ramadan's concerns are valid and relevant to the situation in twenty-first century Britain.

Ramadan is clear that women should themselves play an integral part in ensuring that these problems are dealt with. This is why education becomes so crucial; without education, women cannot study the sacred texts for themselves, and so are unable to help bring a more balanced interpretation of the texts. A particular example is that of the treatment of polygamy within the Qur'an. Ramadan suggests that the context in this topic was discussed was one of unrestricted, unlimited polygamy. He raises the question about the deeper meaning of the Prophet's restriction of polygamy, and imposition (according to some Islamic scholars) of the requirement that the first wife consent to any subsequent marriage. Although he does not state it explicitly, Ramadan implies that the Prophet's restriction was an initial movement whose ultimate goal may perhaps have been exclusive monogamy; an ideal that he is clear requires both men and women to study the relevant texts together to determine.

He does not engage in a detailed discussion of the texts himself, and so it is impossible to be certain as to which texts he has in mind. However, the most commonly cited defense of the practice of polygamy within Islam is this *ayat*: "If you fear that you will not act fairly toward the orphan girls, marry what seems good to you of the women: two, three, or four. But if you fear that you will not be fair, (marry only) one, or what your right (hands) own." (4:3)

---

6. See Bulman and McCourt, "Somali Refugee Women's Experiences"; Cameron and Anderson, "'Circumcision,' Culture and Health-care Provision"; Johnsdotter "Somali women in Western exile."

7. Ansari, *The Infidel Within*, 275.

This is taken as giving permission for marriage of up to four women. It is taken as a corrective in three senses. First, there was a tendency amongst men in pre-Islamic Mecca to marry (have sexual relations with) any orphan girls in their care; this instruction tells them to turn their attentions elsewhere, to older, more suitable women. Second, there was no limit to the number of marriages permitted, whereas here a limit of four is established. Third, there is an expectation that any woman who is married will be treated fairly; if a man cannot do this, he should not marry more than one woman.

Modern Christian readers might question this text on the basis of equality between men and women: why are men permitted to be polygamous but women are not? Christians must recognize that the accounts of the Old Testament, perhaps most notably the sexual relationships of the Patriarchs or Kings David and Solomon, are equally challenging texts to interpret. Moreover, there are parts of the world where people who identify as Christian do engage in polygamous relationships. However, whilst this is the case, it is also true that Jesus only ever condones marriage as a life-long union between one man and one woman, ruling out polygamy as a possibility for Christians, but it is difficult to build a similar case for the absolute prohibition of polygamy within Islam.

The Qur'an does recognize that it is difficult for a man married to several women to treat them equally: "You will not be able to act fairly among the women, even though you are eager (to do so). But do not turn completely away (from one of them) so that you leave her, as it were, in suspense. If you set (things) right and guard (yourselves)—surely God is forgiving, compassionate." (4:129).

This recognition of the difficulty of obeying the earlier injunction to treat all wives fairly may be the reason that, in my experience, devout Muslims living in the UK tend to only have one wife. Although polygamy is illegal in the UK, it would be theoretically possible for a Muslim man to have one wife in the eyes of the law and exclusive relationships with other women that the community recognized as an Islamic marriage, but had no legal basis. Such an arrangement would, inevitably, be kept secret from outsiders, and so it would be difficult to know if it existed. Perhaps these difficulties, and the sensitivities within Muslim society about them, are the reasons Ramadan does not explicitly tackle the topic.

Whether such polygamous relationships are a reality in the UK or not, the challenge of equal treatment of women and men within Islam remains a real one that must be addressed. Ramadan is clear about this, and he also welcomes wider contributions, from those qualified in fields other than the Islamic sciences, arguing in particular for the importance of contributions from the social sciences, from anthropology, history, sociology, and ethnography. In his view, the ultimate focus of any such discourse is on topics of being, dignity, development, freedom, equality, justice, balance, love, and welfare. Ramadan is clear that this is a spiritual imperative, not simply a social one. He argues that the foundational work must concern faith, spirituality, and the quest for meaning before issues of social discrimination and power structures within particular human groups are tackled.

The reason for this concern is that Ramadan believes that the debate is reactionary rather than measured, it will loose sight of what Islam actually teaches. He argues that sustained pressure from Western audiences, who view the clothing choices of devout Muslim women as symbols of oppression and discriminatory submission, has had precisely the opposite effect. Rather than allowing women to make informed, free choices, it has instead led to a negative reaction, whereby more conservative choices are made as an act of resistance against perceived Western cultural imperialism. He is clear that the debate must be about what Islam teaches, not about how to respond to particular cultural norms, however those are perceived. The first stage is to ensure women are respected as equal, that discrimination in the workplace on the basis of gender is eradicated; there must be a reform of social mindsets and dynamics, a movement for justice, equality, and rights. This involves challenging "all formalist dictatorships, both that which imposes the headscarf without belief in the practice coming from the heart and that which imagines all objectified female bodies fit into a size six dress, that which compels women to stay at home for religious reasons and that which sends them back home after the age of forty-five for aesthetic reasons."[8]

Ramadan's central concern is that women are respected as people—that their rights are respected and their needs understood.

## Modest Dress

*Radical Reform* does not discuss Islamic teaching about clothing in much detail. Elsewhere Ramadan argues that Muslims should dress modestly, but simultaneously recognizes that injunctions to modest dress are common

8. Ramadan, *Radical Reform*, 221.

to many religions, and does not prescribe what modest dress must be for a British Muslim.[9] He believes choices made in relation to clothing should be outward manifestations of an inner and personal piety. He is critical of parents who force their daughters to wear headscarves without instilling in those same children the deep personal piety that such a choice ought, in Ramadan's view, to reflect. He also argues that the choice to wear a headscarf is one that a Muslim might arrive at gradually, based on the fact that the injunction to cover oneself was given after fifteen years, rather than in the first days of the revelation to the Prophet.[10] He moreover suggests that Muslim women in the West may wear headscarves as an indication of their faith, but they also dress according to Western fashion trends,[11] and the decision to wear a headscarf should be in no way coerced.[12]

A Muslim woman may wear a headscarf for a wide variety of reasons. Haddad suggests nine possible motivations for wearing a headscarf: religious (obedience to a divine command); psychological (affirming Islamic authenticity, creating a sense of peace); political (protest against an existing political regime); revolutionary (indicating a desire to "Islamicise" society); economic (a sign of affluence); cultural (a sign of chastity and modesty); demographic (a sign of being urbanized); practical (to reduce expenditure on clothing) and domestic (to keep males in the family contented).[13] Furthermore, as Tarlo notes, Muslims wear a wide range of clothing, and the idea of modest dress is by no means exclusively Islamic.[14] She documents how different Muslim women have interpreted the Qur'anic injunctions (notably 24:30–1; 33:59) to modesty, arguing that they are actively engaged in selecting clothing that is both fashionable and in conformity with Islamic standards.

Western Christians do not tend to discuss issues relating to modest dress in much detail, although it is normal in many Christian contexts for women to cover their heads. When I worked in Gloucester, the Afro-Caribbean women who attended the churches I served invariably wore a hat whenever they went outside, and especially when attending a church function of any kind. I will return to the issue of women covering their

9. Ramadan, *The Quest*, 85.
10. Ramadan, *Islam, the West and the Challenge of Modernity*, 53–4, 251–7.
11. Ramadan, *Western Muslims*, 142.
12. Ramadan, *Radical Reform*, 219.
13. Cited by Geaves, *Aspects of Islam*, 233–4.
14. Tarlo, *Visibly Muslim*.

heads later in the chapter, but for the moment simply note that whilst 1 Peter 3:3–4 encourages wives that their beauty should come from their inner selves not their outer adornment, the New Testament says little else specifically about modesty in dress.

## The Mosque

In *Radical Reform*, Ramadan suggests that the role and function of mosques within society is a specific concrete issue where the role and status of women can be discussed in some detail.[15] He recognizes mosques as religious spaces expressing a certain idea of authority, the substance of a discourse, and the distribution of roles. This is nothing new within Islam, but the choices made about welcoming women (or otherwise) are reflective of wider social attitudes and their position within the social structure.

What is of particular significance in the example of the mosque in Ramadan's view is the fact that women were welcome to and active within the Prophet's mosque in Medina, something that is rarely replicated in Islam today. Instead, mosques have become essentially men's places; a reality that Ramadan argues does not correspond to the higher objectives of Islam's message. He recognizes that there are *ahadith* that express the idea that it is preferable for women to pray at home, but regards the counter-argument of the Prophet's own practice and the core tenets of Islam's teaching as indicating that mosques should be open to women. He explains that in the mosque in Medina, men would line up at the front and women behind them, in order to preserve modesty. But they were in the same space, and all were able to express their views.[16]

Ramadan recognizes that the realities of modern life and cultural expectations may mean that it is impossible to go back to a single common space, but this does not mean that men and women could not have equal access to facilities of the same standard. What is especially challenging is that during festivities (notably Ramadan), women's facilities are taken over by men, and the women are expected to pray at home. My own experience confirms this reality. Invariably mosques are almost exclusively male domains. Of the five places that I am aware of where Muslims gather to pray in Gloucester, three are established mosques which make no provision for

15. Ramadan, *Radical Reform*, 221–4.
16. On the development of mosques in the UK, see Gilliat-Ray, *Muslims in Britain*, 181–205.

women, one is a newly established Sufi mosque, which has plans to build a separate women's facility, and one is a prayer room above an Islamic bookshop, where equal provision is made for men and women (one room is available for each gender). This bookshop is the most recently established of the five, reflecting perhaps that more modern Muslim organizations are more concerned to make provision for women. The owners explained to me that although they personally had reservations about women praying outside the home, they recognized that having a prayer space was important for some Muslim women, and so they chose to provide such facilities.

The problem is not just limited to provision of space to pray: mosque councils are invariably exclusively male domains. Until this changes, there will be no real reform of how mosques are run. This is not just for reasons of equality, but also in order to promote the spiritual wellbeing of the whole community. Ramadan suggests that women, more than men, "encourage spiritual, meaning-oriented teaching, rather than formalistic approaches confined to rites, obligations, and prohibitions."[17] Only when women are in governance roles within mosques will this benefit be felt throughout Muslim communities, which in particular need to continue to engage with younger Muslims to ensure they remain committed to the faith.[18]

Christians are in no position to point fingers in relation to issues of religious leadership. Within my own tradition, the Anglican Church, there have been protracted and bitter discussions of the role of women in leadership. One recent positive example of engaging over this issue is *The Gender Agenda* in which two women, one in favor of women's ordination and one against, share their discussion of the issue over several months.[19] Many books have been published arguing for different positions, and it is unnecessary to list them here. The question of engaging young people is one that challenges the churches as much as mosques; people of faith should encourage each other to bring up their children as believers in a world that continually marginalizes all forms of religious belief.

## The Family

The family is crucial within Islam, and Muhammad spoke very highly of mothers in particular. A commonly cited *hadith* (of Al-Tirmidhi) records

17. Ramadan, *Radical Reform*, 223.
18. On this issue, see Gest *Apart*; Lewis *Young, British and Muslim*.
19. Goddard and Hendry, *The Gender Agenda*.

how a man once consulted Muhammad about taking part in a military campaign. The Prophet asked the man if his mother was still living. When told that she was alive, the Prophet said: "(Then) stay with her, for Paradise is at her feet."

The status of women as mothers is high within Islam. However, as Ramadan notes, the pressures on modern family life are immense: "Constituting a balanced, harmonious family and being able to resist the stresses of personality and time require permanent effort; it is a struggle, a *jihad* that cannot be won through normative injunctions but rather by relying on deep understanding of the objectives of married life, parenthood, and love."[20]

This struggle is one that all Muslims should engage in. According to a *hadith* of al-Bayhaqi, the Prophet said that those who marry have achieved "half the religion," reiterating the fact that there is not a strong tradition of singleness or celibacy within Islam. The goals of marriage are both meeting the needs of husband and wife and also conformity with religious and ethical teachings. These goals cannot be reached merely through a formalist adherence to theoretical Islamic understandings, but require a real and wholehearted commitment to living them out in the struggles of daily life.

Ramadan argues for a reform of marriage within the Islamic world. He calls for all those with relevant expertise, including scholars, psychologists, and social workers to engage in this reform together. He expects couples to marry on the basis of love, but expects that love to be nurtured, maintained, and deepened through care and commitment, thoughtfulness, and dialogue, through enabling and equipping couples to weather crises, and grow together in love. Ramadan suggests that Islam does not make marriage compulsory, but that marriage, shared love, and fulfillment, remains "the most natural choice for most people."

He also states it is important to recognize the different pressures and situations that people face compared to previous generations. Fatherhood today is not the same as being a father in previous generations; indeed Ramadan goes so far as to speak of a "crisis of fatherhood," amongst those who are struggling to resolve issues of presence, transmission of faith, relating to the mother, and to authority and the process of children acquiring autonomy. He wants Muslim communities to be honest in engaging with difficult issues; in particular he is concerned that real issues are being hidden by attempts to blame all social ills on female emancipation when the

---

20. Ramadan, *Radical Reform*, 225.

reality is far more complex. Thus he argues that it is laudable that issues of the prohibition of forced marriage, domestic violence, and genital mutilation are being tackled, but although these are pressing concerns, they are not the only concerns. All issues of equality, especially those related to marriage and inheritance rights must be dealt with. Dealing with these problems requires both a deeper reading of texts and a clearer understanding of the realities of daily life and the challenges faced by women, men, and families.

Christians also recognize the challenge of family life in the modern world, and in particular of supporting Christian men. There are specific organizations that champion this, such as Christian Vision for Men[21] and others that work to support Christian families, such as Care for the Family[22] or Relationship Central,[23] to give two British examples.

## WHAT KIND OF FRIENDSHIP?

Ramadan is optimistic about the future. There are some signs of change, of progress being made. Education has been central to the changes that have taken place; where women have access to decent education, they are able to bring about major change, because educated women are able to study texts and learn about their faith, and so are able to establish new relationships with their religion, to offer proposals for how to live faithfully to Islam in the modern world.

Reading about the challenges facing the Muslim community in the UK, there are some echoes and some differences with the Christian community. There are some texts within the Christian scriptures that undoubtedly are problematic for some. Some of these concern family life and others the position of women in leadership within church communities. The household codes, of which Ephesians 5:22–6:5; Colossians 3:18–4:1 and 1 Peter 2:13–3:9 are the most commonly studied, and have been argued by some Christians to promote unfair treatment of women. Others would argue that when read as products of their social setting, they are far more generous than they might at first appear, a style of argument not entirely dissimilar from Ramadan's discussion of polygamy above. The texts on women in leadership, notably 1 Corinthians 14:33–5 and 1 Timothy 2:11–2, have

21. www.cvm.org.uk
22. www.careforthefamily.org.uk
23. www.relationshipcentral.org

## Women: Traditions and Liberation

been subject to much debate, with some arguing on the basis of these texts (and Jesus' male gender) that women should not have formal positions of church leadership. There are many nuances and complexities to this debate, which I will not engage with here. What is striking in the context of this discussion is that the Christian debate, in contrast with the Muslim debate about women and mosques, does not concern access, but a leadership function. Virtually every Christian church in the UK would collapse without the countless thousands of volunteer hours put in by women, something that is not entirely true of mosques (although the role of women in teaching Arabic and Qur'anic recitation to young children must be recognized). Moreover, whilst there are some feminist voices within Islam, such as that documented by Lamptey or Jardim,[24] there are far more within Christianity, such as Rosemary Radford Reuther or Elisabeth Schüssler Fiorenza. Numerous studies examine the role of women within the Bible and argue strongly for the role of women in the church.[25] Here there is a clear difference between Islam and Christianity in the West.

Christians and Muslims have similar views on the importance of family life, on the need to support monogamous married heterosexual couples, and the pressures of bringing up children to believe in an increasingly secular society. This is an area where there can—and should—be greater cooperation between people of faith. Education is another, closely related area, where again common concerns are arguably as great as doctrinal and theological differences. Christians may want to encourage Muslims to allow women greater freedom to pray and to be active in practicing their religion, and perhaps the best way to do that is to work together to support family life and education for all religious believers in a society where it is becoming increasingly hard to be a committed person of faith. Christians will want to speak out against hate crimes against Muslims, and in particular to challenge the fact that the majority of anti-Muslim hate crime is committed by men against women who are visibly dressed as Muslims.[26]

---

24. Jardim, *Recovering the Female Voice*; Lamptey, *Never Wholly Other*.
25. Such as Williams, *God Remembered Rachel*.
26. Allen, *Maybe We Are Hated*.

# 8

# Ecology and Economy

IN THE COURSE OF his discussion of issues relating to ecology and the economy, Tariq Ramadan is quite strident in his condemnation of the dearth of reflection amongst Muslims about respecting the environment or about how animals should be treated, claiming that such thought "is virtually nonexistent in contemporary Islamic intellectual discourse."[1] He regards this as a serious problem, because it reflects how Islamic intellectual debate has lost touch with reality. His concern is that contemporary Islamic intellectual discourse concerns itself with religion divorced from creation and all human activities, when in his view the two are inseparable. He argues we should see the whole of the created order as a revelation of the divine, and that recognition of creation as revealing God ought to lead us to a reform of our attitudes towards the natural world, and so to a reform of the economy, which he regards as overly focused on economic production and "the mad logic of economic growth at all costs." He bases this view on that fact the Qur'an speaks of creation in this way:

> Surely in the creation of the heavens and the earth, and (in) the alternation of the night and the day, (there are) signs indeed for those with understanding, who remember God, whether standing or sitting or (lying) in their sides, and reflect on the creation of the heavens and the earth: 'Our Lord, You have not created this in

---

1. Ramadan, *Radical Reform*, 233. There are some discussions of ecological issues from an Islamic perspective, with Abdul-Matin, *Green Deen* being one notable example.

vain. Glory to You! Guard us against the punishment of the Fire'
(3:190–1).

We shall show them Our signs in the skies and in themselves, until it becomes clear to them that it is the truth. Is it not sufficient in (regard to) your Lord that He is a witness over everything? (41:53)

In his explanatory notes on 41:53, Droge comments that "skies," literally "horizons," is said to refer (prophetically) to future Muslim victories in various lands, but argues that it probably refers to the theme of the signs of God's power and providence as manifested in the sky. He likewise adds that "in themselves" most likely refers to signs of God's power and providence as manifested in creation and in the reproduction of humans.[2]

The problem Ramadan identifies in contemporary Islamic discourse is an over focus on details and symptoms without any effort to engage in the detailed work necessary to address the underlying concerns. Ramadan finds a marked contrast in the life of Muhammad, who was deeply concerned about the created order. Ramadan regards Muhammad as modeling perfect concern for both people and nature, setting the example for Muslims to follow.

Ramadan suggests that Muhammad was concerned to respect nature and avoid waste, citing a *hadith* of Ahmad and Ibn Majah that one day the Prophet saw one of his followers, Sa'd ibn Abi Waqqas performing ritual ablutions and scolded him for wasting water as he washed himself. For Ramadan, although water is central to cleansing rituals, it must never be merely thought of as a means to the end of spiritual edification, but the correct use of water (with respect, without waste) is a spiritual end in and of itself. Concern for the natural world extends also into the animal kingdom. Ramadan cites a *hadith* of Bukhari and Muslim that records a story the Prophet told about a man walking along a road in very hot weather. The man came across a well, and climbed down to quench his thirst. When he came back up, he saw a dog panting with thirst, and said to himself, "This dog is as thirsty as I was," and went back down the well a second time, filling his shoe with water and climbing out, with the shoe between his teeth. He gave the water to the dog to drink, and as a result, Muhammad concluded, God rewarded him, forgiving his sins.

What is especially striking about this *hadith* is that it was a dog that was provided for. In Arab Muslim culture, both in the seventh century,

2. Droge, *The Qur'an*, 322.

and even today, dogs are regarded as unclean animals, not one to associate with. Yet here care for a dog is a deed that receives a great reward, emphasizing the fact that care of creation is of paramount importance. The case Ramadan is building is that true religious observance will necessarily lead to a concern for creation over and above a concern for precise obedience and clinically correct orthopraxy. He suggests that many other stories could be told to emphasize the same point, but rather than continue to speak generally, he turns to focus on five specific issues: ritual slaughter, growth and sustainable development, an Islamic economy, *halal* consumption, and the planet, poverty, and genetically modified organisms.

## RITUAL SLAUGHTER

In Ramadan's view,[3] the present debate over ritual slaughter clearly illustrates the betrayal of the fundamental message of Islam and the confusion between means and ends that exists within the faith. The debate has gotten bogged down in determining when, and in what conditions, an animal slaughtered by Muslims (or non-Muslims), with what technique or equipment, can be considered to be *halal*. Questions such as whether the animal can be stunned, what constitutes an animal being alive before it is killed, the religious beliefs of the slaughterer, and whether the sacrifice formula must be actually spoken or simply played on a recording, are typical of the debate. Ramadan does not dismiss these questions, recognizing them to be both important and meaningful, but suggests that wider questions about consumption are being overlooked.

In his view, it is not simply a question of ensuring that the appropriate sacrificial formula (*bismillah al rahman al rahim*, "in the name of God, the compassionate, the merciful") is said as an animal's throat is cut. The concern must be for the welfare of the animal as well. Ramadan quotes a *hadith* of Bukhari that recounts how Muhammad saw a man who had immobilized an animal which he was about to kill, and was sharpening his knife in front of it. Muhammad intervened, saying, "Do you want to make it die twice? Why didn't you sharpen your knife away from the animal's view before immobilizing it?" From this, and the Prophet's injunction that people strive to be the best they can be at their profession and tasks, Ramadan extrapolates that for someone whose task is to slaughter animals, there is a religious expectation that animals will be respected as living beings,

---

3. Ramadan, *Radical Reform*, 236–8.

their needs provided for, and they would only be slaughtered when necessary, with all unnecessary suffering avoided. It therefore cannot be enough to simply say *bismillah al rahman al rahim* and slaughter an animal that has been mistreated during its lifetime. In Ramadan's view, such practice as "an anomaly and a betrayal of the message" that Muhammad brought. He supports this with a further *hadith* (of an-Nasa'i), that the Prophet stated "He who kills a sparrow or any bigger animal without right will have to account for it to God on Judgment Day." Animals are to be cared for and respected, and although the means of slaughter are important, this is by no means the sum of the debate. Ramadan summarizes his own views thus: "Being obsessed by the techniques of *halal* and *a fortiori* saying nothing and proposing nothing about the issue of the outrageous treatment of animals in our societies marked by overconsumption and excessive productivity (in some factory-breeding farms, in slaughterhouses), as well as the ill-treatment of animals in poorer societies, all this is most illogical, astounding, and simply deranged."[4]

The consumption of *halal* food cannot, in Ramadan's view, be reduced simply to technicalities about slaughter. He is clear that wasting food and mistreating animals are both examples of people failing to remain faithful to the teaching of Islam, and goes so far as to argue that respecting the lives of living animals is more important than techniques used in slaughter. For Ramadan, this whole debate summarizes the problems with contemporary Islamic practice, which he summarizes as an obsession with form regardless of substance, confusion of means and ends, and over determining norms while neglecting meaning.

The slaughter of animals according to Islamic stipulations is a topic of perennial debate in the British media. There are those who are concerned about animal welfare, and who argue that any form of slaughter that precludes stunning is unnecessarily cruel. In particular, some vets will argue that however quickly an animal's throat is cut, it will experience pain—a pain that could be avoided if the animal were stunned prior to slaughter. These specific animal welfare concerns are important ones, but I concur with Ramadan's point that over-focus on the final minutes of an animal's life, with no discussion of how that animal is raised, misses the point of the debate. If we are to concern ourselves with animal welfare, then we must pay attention to the entirety of an animal's life. Ramadan returns to this specific issue when he discusses *halal* consumption, so for the moment I

---

4. Ibid., 237.

will simply note the holistic approach to animal welfare rather than a narrow focus on the final minutes of an animal's life, and keep any engagement with Christian commentators for the subsequent section.

## GROWTH AND SUSTAINABLE DEVELOPMENT

Perhaps surprisingly for a non-Muslim audience, Ramadan begins his discussion of the issues around growth and sustainable development with a discussion of fasting during the month of Ramadan.[5] He summarizes the essence of fasting as taking a break from normal practice, a chance to reflect on meaning and essentials, a chance to break the routines and habits of consumption and of competition to acquire more. The problem, as he sees it, is that this essence has been lost. Rather than be a month of spiritual awakening, a time when faith comes alive, the month of Ramadan has become itself overtaken by consumption and consumerism. Rather than consume less and better (in terms of conscience and quality), what happens, especially in Muslim majority countries, is that people simply consume less during the day but far more during the night, consuming without moderation, even with total abandon. Ramadan regards this as "another example of formalist perversion: norm and form are maintained while the religious practice's ethical goals are lost."[6]

Having worked with Muslims in the UK for a number of years, it is noticeable that for some the month of Ramadan is a time to become nocturnal, when they stop work, or avoid any unnecessary activity during the day, while trying to maintain a semblance of a normal life by being primarily active at night. Others strive to fast while maintaining their normal daily employment, something that I have watched with enormous respect. The challenge for Muslims is to ensure that fasting during Ramadan, and then celebrating Eid at the end, is primarily a spiritual exercise. Much the same could be said of contemporary Christians in the season of Advent leading up to Christmas. How many of us forget to contemplate the return of Jesus to judge the world because we are so caught up in ensuring we have bought presents for all our friends and family and have enough food to consume in excess on Christmas Day and the week that follows? As the introduction to the Anglican liturgy for Advent observes, Advent is a season of expectation

---

5. Ibid., 239–42.
6. Ibid., 239.

and preparation in which we remember both Christ's birth and also meditate on the four last things: death, judgment, heaven, and hell.[7]

What is also surprising, for Ramadan, is the lack of formal critique of these problems from within Islam. While the West is condemned for its hedonism and excessive consumption, the perversion of the Ramadan fast passes almost without comment. Moreover, there is little sustained reflection on how to develop poorer and less industrialized societies in a fashion that respects the dignity of individual human beings and promotes solidarity between them. There ought, Ramadan argues, to be sustained attempts at developing Islamic models of development that are rigorous and realistic enough to be sustained in real world situations.

In his view, the whole economic basis of the current world order is open to question and debate. The solution cannot come, Ramadan proposes, simply from tweaking the current model of sustainable development; fundamental questions must be asked of whether development motivated primarily by technical and economic growth is the only possible model for society, or whether alternatives can be developed. The oil-producing countries, many of which have Muslim-majority societies, are one group that ought to take a lead in developing different concepts for industry and consumption. The problem is enormous: ecological disasters, social collapse, illiteracy, and poverty to name but a few. Radical solutions are needed.

Ramadan would find many allies amongst Christians in this struggle. Rowan Williams has written on the importance of "changing the myths we live by," arguing that the dominant modes by which we understand the world and ourselves are not sustainable in the long term. The contemporary myth (by which he means controlling narrative) that creation is a resource to be used and economic production and increasing wealth are the highest human goals leads inexorably to destruction. We need a different myth to live by. Williams states that creation is itself an act of communication, an address that expresses intelligence and asks for an intelligent response. He describes creation as "an act of divine self-giving," which must be received from God with blessing and thanksgiving and offered back to God with blessing and gratitude.[8] In Williams' view, how we engage with creation reflects how we engage with God. God's self-giving in the gift of creation should challenge us to respect and steward creation carefully and wisely. Quoting Eastern Christian thought, he argues that "Everything that hap-

---

7. Common Worship, *Times and Seasons*, 33.
8. Williams, *Faith in the Public Square*, 177.

pens to exist, everything that belongs in the interlocking pattern of the intelligible world, is, and is the way it is, in virtue of this underlying reality which is God's giving."[9] This is the Christian myth that the world needs to hear. Although public lobbying and campaigning are important, what is needed above all else is the living out of a different myth, showing the truth of the relationship between creator and creation, and especially the role of humanity in stewarding creation.[10]

Michael Northcott agrees with Rowan Williams that we need to rediscover the interconnectedness of creation.[11] He deconstructs the post-enlightenment myth of inanimate nature open to exploitation by dominant humanity, explaining its origins and its fallacy in great detail. For Northcott, climate change is an immanent catastrophe, the impact of which we may already be too late to prevent. Change will only come, he believes, if we no longer think of the planet as a dead resource to exploit, but as an interconnected network of living beings, the wellbeing of which we are ultimately responsible for. Northcott's book is clear on the complexity of the problems. Citing the example of the need to move away from fossil fuel consumption he notes that our entire economy is premised on oil, and that the value of oil reserves alone is roughly equivalent to the combined value of all the houses and factories on the planet. If this is written off through a decision to stop extracting and consuming oil, then it would trigger a global economic crisis of immense proportions; billions of us have public and private pensions invested in part in energy companies, and losing this would be disastrous.[12] It is not the case that we can simply say the rich are greedy and they should stop; we are all caught up in a complex oil-dependent web from which we must swiftly extract ourselves before it is too late.

## AN ISLAMIC ECONOMY?

Although the problems are enormous, the solution does not, Ramadan argues, lie in establishing an "Islamic economy" because he does not think it exists, any more than an "Islamic medicine" exists.[13] Rather, there are Islamic ethical principles that have a strong influence of how economic

9. Ibid., 178.
10. Ibid., 183.
11. Northcott, *A Political Theology of Climate Change*.
12. Northcott, *A Political Theology*.
13. Ramadan, *Radical Reform*, 242–8.

and financial activities are conducted. Three key principles are those of *riba* (rejecting interest), *zakat* (a purifying social tax) and *musharakah* (risk sharing). As with the other issues discussed in this chapter, Ramadan's central concerns are first, that form is not maintained at the expense of substance and second, that reform is real. Applying Islamic principles to economic activity cannot simply be a cosmetic exercise, one where aspects of the liberal market economy are adapted to give them a veneer of Islamic orthodoxy and respectability. Thus it is not enough for a firm to produce products that are classified as *halal*, while at the same time "aspiring to the same profit levels and soulless consumerism" of every other capitalist organization.[14]

Ramadan wants to draw a clear distinction between economic activity that generates a legitimate and fair profit and a global economic system that he regards as being "blindly and madly driven by the accumulation of wealth, growth, quantitative development, privatization, and the commercial exploitation of beings, good and services."[15] He cites the growth of so-called *shariah*-compliant Islamic finance products offered by the great international banks such as HSBC or Crédit Suisse as an example of the failure to tackle these issues. These financial products are not offered out of a genuine desire to apply Islamic principles to economic activity, but as a new potential market for a global business eager to generate greater profits.

The problem is, simply put, that there is no viable alternative to the dominant neo-liberal economic model. Whilst the Islamic world may criticize the charging of interest, the trade in stocks and shares, manipulation and speculation of currency, and the injustices of international trade, the harsh reality is that the economic order forces itself on everyone. Yet despite the current lack of a viable alternative, Ramadan is clear that there must be a radical reform of the mind-set and the philosophical and ethical fundamentals of the economic order. Neither skepticism nor criticism should deter hard thinking and tough questioning. This, he claims, is not "wide-eyed dreaming" nor is it advocating Marxism, but an honest reflection on the damage caused by our current economic practices. Ramadan is certain that change must come, if not from principled objections, then because of the crises that flow from the neo-liberal capitalist model, which

---

14. Ibid., 243.
15. Ibid., 244.

he lists as "global warming, rampant poverty, massive migration, wars, terrorism, and other still unknowable disasters."[16]

Ramadan's is by no means the sole voice raising these concerns. But what he finds especially challenging is that only a small minority of Muslims are raising these concerns, despite the fact that he regards Islam as being eminently suited to providing the basis for such reform work. A true devotion to Islam ought to lead to a reform that is centered on welfare, freedom, and solidarity with others, as well as a reflection of humanity's dignity, balance, and autonomy as a being and a subject. The type of reform he envisages is not simply a tweaking of existing models to ensure that neoliberal capitalist production can be technically classed as *halal*. Rather, he is advocating "long-term, thorough detailed studies, a global vision to be spelled out in detail," which will enable a network of local groups to all resist the expansion and power of the capitalist machine.[17]

Ramadan envisages a two-stage process of reform. The first is a change of thinking: the mind-set of many must change to more accurately reflect a true Islamic ethic. The second is more practical. Local and international real-world experiences of managing alternative projects, ethical investments, banking cooperatives, small banks that offer microcredit and other such initiatives should be shared and replicated. Of particular importance in the process is the need to share the wealth of experience from the global south, where there are many small projects, whose successes are not widely disseminated, and so their experience cannot be easily learnt from. Ramadan also calls for all those who are engaged in resisting the economic order within the West to work together, urging Muslims in particular to work with others in the West who are resisting the dominant Western economic system.

Rowan Williams' reflections on this topic sound a remarkably similar note to Ramadan's. Williams describes money as a metaphor, arguing that our monetary transactions bring out features of the human condition and tell us something of how we see our relationship with God.[18] His point is that money is not good or bad in and of itself, but that what we do with it tells us about how we view ourselves, other people, the created order, and God. Williams points out that the term "economy" has its origins in the word for "housekeeping," and that a household is where life is lived in com-

---

16. Ibid., 246.
17. Ibid., 247.
18. Williams, *Faith in the Public Square*, 225.

mon, and housekeeping is "guaranteeing that this common life has some stability about it that allows the members of the household to grow and flourish and act in useful ways."[19] In a similar vein to Ramadan, Williams is not arguing for the creation of a specifically Christian economy. He is clear that theology does not answer specific economic concerns. What theology can do, however, is offer a "robust definition of what human well-being looks like and what the rationale is for human life well-lived in common."[20] In essence the point is that Christian ethical reflection on consumption, on fair employment, on care for creation, and a host of related topics, will all inform the economic model that is developed and deployed throughout the world, an idea equally present in recent comments from the current Archbishop of Canterbury.[21]

## HALAL CONSUMPTION?

In his discussion of *halal* consumption, Ramadan understands consumption (of food, beverages, clothing, housing, transportation, entertainment) as revealing the priorities and general philosophy of the consumer.[22] What we buy, and how we purchase it, reveals the nature of our religious beliefs. With this in mind, Ramadan questions the growth of the *halal* market, asking whether it is in fact true to the foundational principles of Islam. In Ramadan's view, those involved in producing purportedly *halal* products are guilty of failing to question "the productivist, mercantilist, materialistic points of reference and state of mind" that characterizes much of the neoliberal capitalist machine.[23] He laments the fact that little consideration is given to the "squandering of natural resources, to the exploitation of men, women, and children, to the outrageous treatment of animals."[24] When the only motives are profit and a veneer of Islamic respectability, Ramadan does not consider the goods and services produced to be genuinely *halal*. His criticism is strong, as he complains that, "Fast food is profitable, therefore Islamic, *halal* fast-food restaurants are put into operation, from McDonald's to other famous brands. Coke dominates the soft drink market, so

19. Ibid., 227.
20. Ibid., 228.
21. Welby, "The Good Economy."
22. Ramadan, *Radical Reform*, 248–52.
23. Ibid., 247.
24. Ibid., 247.

a line of products labeled as "Cola" emerges (Mecca Cola, Zem Zem Cola, Medina Cola) to recall the "taste" of the parent company's product while they are alleged to resist the actions of the foreign company or constitute an alternative!"[25]

Although the examples may at first glance seem relatively trivial, for Ramadan the underlying problems they identify are quite serious. The logic of such products indicate, he suggests, a veneer of "Islamity" covering objectives that have little serious ethical concern, and are indifferent to the "collateral damage produced by such economic processes."[26] In the same way as people are satisfied that meat is *halal* if the animal has been slaughtered according to strict principles regardless of how it was treated during its life, so equally little thought is given to how workers are treated in producing the *halal* goods which they consume. Ramadan's clearest example is Fulla, a *hijab* clad doll, "an Islamized duplicate of the Barbie doll complete with a line of accessories that, like it, is made in China."[27] His point is not that Fulla is not an Islamic product, but that it is a symptom of the subversion and conquest of Islam by the capitalist system. This is not to say he is against children playing, or having dolls, but that he regards Fulla more as a cynical exploitation of a marketing opportunity than as an expression of an authentic Islamic faith.

This is one example of the fact that fundamental issues emerge from simple day-to-day life choices. Returning to the example of *halal* slaughter of animals, Ramadan offers two options, asking which is considered ethically more Islamic, more *halal*. The first is a chicken that was mistreated while alive, never seen the light of day, and was slaughtered according to Islamic norms with the ritual formula. The second is a chicken raised according to strict organic food criteria in a healthy, free-range environment and slaughtered without any form of ritual formula being proclaimed over it. Ramadan suggests that in an ideal world, a chicken consumed by a Muslim would be organic, free-range, and slaughtered accorded to ritual stipulations. But in the absence of these, he regards the second option of the organic bird as *halal* in essence and principle, and suggests that Muslims should buy this chicken and simply add, before eating, the usual formula *Bismillahi ar Rahman ar Rahim* themselves. Concern for the welfare of

---

25. Ibid., 249.
26. Ibid., 250.
27. Ibid., 250.

the animal is thus more important than satisfying technical requirements about slaughter.

On this point, Ramadan may gain a sympathetic hearing from at least some of those who oppose *halal* slaughter. I am unclear after reading Ramadan on this topic as to whether he would prefer to stun an animal prior to slaughter in order to eliminate any experience of pain. One could expect on the basis of the *hadith* quoted above, about the importance of sharpening a knife prior to slaughter out of sight of the animal to be killed, that Ramadan would not oppose the stunning of animals prior to slaughter. But he does not state this explicitly, so that may be reading too much into his argument.

As a Christian I would oppose the unnecessary exploitation of animals, and argue they must be treated as decently as possible. Such ideals do raise complex problems: intensive food production is, obviously, far more productive than extensive. It takes far less time and resource to raise a chicken for slaughter in a battery farm than an organic, free-range one. Therefore, a decision to rethink how much meat we eat and how much we are prepared to pay for it must be an integral part of any discussion about animal welfare. Moreover, questions need to be asked about how much meat we should consume and the environmental impact of all forms of meat production. Ramadan's point about joined-up, holistic thinking about problems is an important one that Christians should apply to their own views on consumerism.

Ramadan's principles can be applied to all forms of consumption. His objective is ensuring that contemporary Muslims have their consciences "awakened and redirected on such issues."[28] This, he recognizes, is no simple task. It requires detailed and sophisticated reflection by many specialists, including textual scholars, scientists, and economists, to build an ethics of consumption that is consistent with the Islamic principles of welfare, freedom, solidarity, dignity, balance, and autonomy that he has outlined throughout this work. Although it will be difficult, Ramadan is clear it is necessary to free the Muslim world from its current position, where injustice is twinned with hypocrisy, and Islam is misrepresented.

Christian Biblical scholars have developed a number of arguments that support and enhance the point that Ramadan makes. I will give two representative examples, one from the Old Testament and one from the New Testament. In his study of Old Testament laws on wealth and poverty,

28. Ibid., 251.

David Baker argues that they teach much of contemporary relevance.[29] First, property ownership is understood as a divinely given right, and therefore members of the covenant community may not deprive others of their property. On a related note, material possessions are of far lesser value than human life, and all ownership of goods and property includes responsibilities for wise use. Second, those on the margins of society, notably slaves, widows, and orphans are to be cared for generously. Third, people should be honest, just, and generous in all their dealings with their fellows. Baker suggests that the following verse from Deuteronomy summarizes the entire ethic of the Old Testament: "You shall not be hard-hearted or tight-fisted toward your poor brother. Rather, open your hand generously to him" (Deuteronomy 15:7b-8a). This is, I think, an injunction Ramadan would agree with wholeheartedly.

Turning to the New Testament, Brian Rosner examines the Pauline phrase "greed is idolatry."[30] He suggests idolatry is the most serious of sins, because it is the distinguishing mark of those who do not know God. To equate greed with idolatry therefore elevates it to an equally serious position. Rosner explains the metaphor of greed as idolatry is teaching that having a strong desire to acquire and keep for yourself more and more money and material possessions is an attack on God's exclusive right to human love and devotion, trust and confidence, and service and obedience. Although one might argue that other vices are equally idolatrous, with sexual immorality being one possible example, for Rosner, greed is at the heart of all of these, because other vices are all rooted in greed. Modern hedonistic society sorely needs to learn this lesson, and to replace the vice of idolatrous greed with the holy virtue of a desire to seek first God's kingdom and his righteousness.

Michael Northcott does not engage in exegesis of Biblical texts, but he is clear that consumption patterns must change if we are to survive as a species. He bases his argument on a Christian view of the world as a gift of God for which humans are responsible. He outlines the complexity of the problem by reference to the Jevons paradox. The Jevons paradox, named after William Jevons, who first identified it in relation to coal consumption in the nineteenth century, is that energy efficiency savings did not result in less energy consumption. Instead, greater energy efficiency had the same impact as cheaper energy: it promotes more energy consumption because

---

29. Baker, *Tight Fists or Open Hands?*
30. Rosner, *Greed as Idolatry.*

"the economic rewards of activities that would previously have been more costly are enhanced by energy efficiency, which lowers the price of energy while increasing the rewards gained from using it."[31]

Therefore, while Northcott does advocate local action to reduce energy consumption, his main concern is that unless fossil fuels remain in the ground, net consumption will only continue to increase exponentially, with catastrophic results for life on our planet. His main contention is that however much energy is saved in Europe and in Northern America, this will be more than offset by rapidly increasing consumption in China and India. The only possible change, he believes, is a radical shift in what is consumed, to a post-carbon global economy.

These are but three possible examples of how Christians have developed serious ethical reflections on consumption in a fashion that is similar to that which Ramadan advocates. Although two of these particular examples involve a close study of particular texts and are not wide-ranging in the same fashion as Ramadan's own study, nevertheless, they advocate similar goals and changes in patterns of behavior.

## THE PLANET, POVERTY, AND GENETICALLY MODIFIED ORGANISMS (GMOS)

Ramadan's main concern in this section is not to implement isolated Islamic laws, but to reform the whole system of Islamic thought, so that it is more suitable for the twenty-first century.[32] He recognizes the complexity of even attempting such a process, noting that so many of the issues are interrelated and there are no clear or simple solutions. He lists a few examples, beginning with the devastation of the natural world, primarily by the richer, industrialized nations who squander natural resources and pollute the planet. What is especially lamentable is that it is the poorer nations who are most affected by the resultant climate change which they themselves did not cause. These are the nations affected by droughts, desertification, increased flooding, decreased agricultural productivity, and rising sea levels.

These are big issues, and require big solutions that deal with issues of economics and consumption as much as those of concern for the natural world. The challenge for the contemporary Muslim conscience, Ramadan suggests, is thus to make "a comprehensive, earnest, far-reaching, realistic,

31. Northcott, *A Political Theology*, 123.
32. Ramadan, *Radical Reform*, 252–8.

and efficient contribution about the educational, economic, and ecological policies that would make it possible to reform the situation and better respect the dignity of Men and nature."[33]

These reforms must be real and long lasting; there is a danger, Ramadan persuasively argues, that catchphrases like "sustainable development" can be just as much a smokescreen for Western economies as *halal* is for Muslim consumers. The changes cannot simply be at the surface level, but must involve radical change. Rather than produce an exhaustive—and exhausting—list of every single problem that must be faced, Ramadan instead simply calls for a change of mind-set, a development of a renewed spirituality that takes care of creation more seriously. The case he makes is remarkably similar to that made by Northcott.

Islam has the resources to contribute to this renewal, of which the injunction to *zakat* is but one example. There ought to be an economic and ethical strategy both for collecting *zakat* and for ensuring it reaches those who need it most. The Qur'an stipulates that the poor do have rights to the wealth of the rich: "Surely the ones who guard (themselves) will be in (the midst of) gardens and springs, taking whatever their Lord has given them. Surely before (this) they were doers of good. Little of the night would they sleep, and in the mornings they would ask for forgiveness, and in their wealth (there was) a due (portion) for the beggar and the outcast." (51:15–9)

The expectation is thus that everyone's needs are provided for. Arguably, there is a strand of New Testament teaching that advocates an even more radical equality. Luke's Gospel is full of stories that warn of how wealth prohibits engagement with God. Thus after he meets with Jesus, Zacchaeus gives half his possessions to the poor and repays anyone he has defrauded four times what was lost (Luke 19:1–10). Jesus tells parables about the dangers of wealth. In one, the rich fool keeps building bigger barns, and concentrates on storing his possessions instead of getting in to right relationship with God (Luke 12:16–21). In another, a different rich man ignores the poor beggar Lazarus at his gate, and finds himself in eternal torment (Luke 16:19–31). Jesus gave the same warning to others: the rich young ruler refuses to part with his possessions, and so is unable to enter the kingdom of God (Luke 18:18–30).

None of us can live as isolated individuals; both Islam and Christianity expect people to care for each other, and to put others' needs above their own rights. Moreover, both religions expect people to recognize what God

---

33. Ibid., 254.

## Ecology and Economy

has given them as a gift and treat it accordingly. As Rowan Williams notes, texts such as Leviticus 25:23 regards us as foreign and temporary tenants on a soil that belongs to God. We are stewards of creation, and our task is to draw out potential treasures from within the natural world and to use creation to nourish humanity without so damaging the balance of nature that it cannot repair itself.[34] We are to care for what we have been given, and not take more than we need.

The final issue Ramadan discusses in this chapter of *Radical Reform* is that of genetically modified organisms (GMOs).[35] He regards them as a further symptom of the problem of over-focus on production and the confusion of means and ends. Ramadan suggests that traditional agriculture, if sufficiently protected and more fairly distributed, would be able to supply the needs of every human being on the planet. However, these agricultural methods have been unfairly distorted by the demands of richer economies, leading to demands for more productive crops and the increasing use of GMOs. GMOs have, in his view, been rushed out too quickly and widely, without sufficient care and attention being paid to potential impact on the natural world, especially biodiversity, and on human health. Ramadan thinks it is especially telling that the rapidly expanding economies of China and India have made great use of GMOs, arguing that it indicates the demands of competitiveness and capitalism have once again dictated an unsafe and unsustainable agenda.

Ramadan laments the fact that contemporary Muslim consciences have not really engaged with these issues, and that even textual scholars and leading religious thinkers do not tackle issues of environmental concern or ethical consumption choices. He wants to see Muslim ethical reflection that has a real impact on practical, day-to-day issues, not simply isolated religious concerns. He wants Muslims to live as witnesses to their faith and believes how they tackle issues of poverty, economic injustice and climate change should be central to that testimony.

## WHAT KIND OF FRIENDSHIP?

Although I have cited a number of Christian authors in this chapter whose views complement those of Tariq Ramadan, it is probably fair to say that although some Christians are very engaged with the issues tackled here,

---

34. Williams, *Faith in the Public Square*, 186–8.
35. Ramadan, *Radical Reform*, 256–8.

many more are not. Christian consciences are in as much need of awakening to the urgency and scale of the problems faced by our planet, for it is only with a collective desire to change the myth we live by and the idols we worship that any real, lasting change will happen. This is another area where Christians and Muslims can—and should—work together for the good of our planet.

# 9

# Society, Education, and Power

THERE'S AN OLD JESUIT saying: "Give me a boy until he is seven, and I will give you the man." The point is that the early, formative years of one's life are crucial for the direction of your whole life. Education is therefore central to any work of reform. Ramadan is convinced that his call for reform will have the greatest impact on the direction of education and political management, especially within the Muslim majority world. He suggests that many countries within the Muslim majority world are in a state of "deep, general crisis." These reflections were written before the Arab Spring, and the unrest that has occurred in recent years would certainly support this contention.

Ramadan does not think he has all of the answers to the problems that the Muslim world faces, but he is clear that much needs to be done. The status quo is not acceptable, and many things that have been taken for granted should, he suggests, be subject to fundamental and searching questions. While he does not claim to have all the answers, Ramadan is clear about what he is setting out to achieve. He wishes to begin the transition that is the necessary precursor to reform. He wants to equip Muslims in the West especially with the "intellectual and methodological means to think and achieve necessary reform." He does not see this as stepping away from the resources of the Qur'an and *ahadith*. Indeed, he regards his work as returning to the heart of the message of Islam, achieving a coherence of thought and life in the modern world, building "bridges between the revealed Book and the Book of the Universe."[1]

Reform must happen, and Ramadan argues it must happen in as open and transparent a fashion as possible. Reform cannot remain in the hands of the elite, but all Muslims must be empowered and equipped to engage in the renewal of their faith for the twenty-first century. In his final case study chapter of *Radical Reform*, Ramadan discusses seven specific themes under the broad heading of society, education, and power.[2] They are religion and politics; public sphere, private sphere and rights; laws, power and civil society; the Islamic penal code; education; democracy and media; and powers and counterpowers. I will work through each of them in turn.

## RELIGION AND POLITICS

In his discussion of religion and politics,[3] Ramadan outlines two overly simplistic understandings of the relationship between religion and politics. He classifies these as the "Western" view that religion and politics have nothing to do with each other, and the view of some thinkers within Islam who claim there is no distinction between religion and politics. Both, he suggests, are not especially accurate caricatures. That is to say, it is not true to say either that religion and politics are identical or that they are unrelated.

One cannot argue religion never impacts politics, Ramadan suggests, giving the example that France is as culturally Roman Catholic as China is culturally Confucian. In his view, what matters is not whether there is a relationship between religion and politics, as he argues there always is, but having a clear knowledge of the type of relationship and how it should be considered. The issue comes down to whom holds what type of authority. The situation is more complex in Islam than in Christianity, as there is no institutional body within Islam that manages religious affairs in a fashion analogous to the structures of the Roman Catholic or Anglican churches (to give but two Christian examples). But even if there are no institutional bodies, there are people who hold different types of power, and the question therefore remains: who holds power and is it legitimate for them to do so?

---

1. Ramadan, *Radical Reform*, 260.
2. Ibid., 259–92.
3. Ibid., 261–6.

## Society, Education, and Power

Ramadan is clear that there must be a clear separation of two types of power: the power of religious dogma and that of political thought. A separation is necessary because, he argues, political pluralism is endangered when a religious power, whose legitimacy is seen as transcendent, is imposed by a "dogmatic mind deaf to other people's beliefs." Here Ramadan is clearly challenging the political structures of certain countries within the Muslim majority world, although when one takes a historical view, it is clear that the challenge applies equally to many other countries as well. He argues that a dogmatic mind does not necessarily have to be religious: it could equally well be Marxist, communist, or aggressively secularist. His concern is that there should be a separation of religious and political authority, to enable both the religious and political sphere to flourish.

Ramadan argues that Islam does distinguish between religion and politics, and this is seen in the distinction between divine revelation and human decisions. Divine revelation, notably of the Qur'an, concerns religious dogmas that all who would identify as Muslim are called to subscribe to. In this area of life, truth is imposed, an existing standard to be conformed to. By contrast, Ramadan suggests that in the sphere of social affairs, that is of politics, then there are a range of possibilities within the limits of what is clearly prohibited by textual and scholarly consensus. Thus, in the sphere of religion, truth is fixed and there is far less leeway than in the sphere of politics, where a number of acceptable options are available, and human ingenuity and creativity are given much greater freedom.

This is not a new distinction within Islam, but one that has a long heritage. Ramadan is clear that early works of Islamic jurisprudence clearly distinguish between worship (*al-ibadat*) and social affairs (*al-mu'amalat*). Thus there is a clear difference within Islamic thought between religion as practiced and religion as it influences political and social concerns. The problem is that this distinction has been lost in more recent times. Ramadan suggests the main reason for this deficiency is the experience of colonization and its aftermath: the need to distinguish Islam from political, economic, and cultural imperialism meant that Islam's fundamental otherness was insisted upon and it became a monolithic block opposing all else in order to survive and maintain a distinct identity. He therefore blames the recent experience of outside influences for the Islamic world forgetting to distinguish between religion and politics. He summarizes his point by arguing that the "Western equation *secularization = freedom = religious pluralism = democracy*" has no equivalent in Muslim-majority societies, where the experience has more been *"secularization = colonialism = de-Islamization = dictatorship."*[4] This is a deep wound that will take a long time to heal, and requires much reflection by Islamic scholars and intellectuals on how to maintain a clear and coherent faith in a politically pluralist and religiously diverse global society.

In his discussion of *Faith Communities in a civil society* Rowan Williams argues that, "The Church is most credible when least preoccupied with its security and most engaged with the human health of its environment; and to say 'credible' here is not to say 'popular,' since engagement with this human health may run sharply against a prevailing consensus."[5] Williams' point is that the Church must, and should, be engaged in the political sphere, and should be doing so not primarily out of personal interest or a desire for self-promotion, but rather out of a sacrificial giving of self and a desire to seek the good of all, regardless of faith conviction. Christians also have a difficult time negotiating the relationship between religion and politics. Religion and politics are therefore two distinct, but related spheres. Religious convictions may drive political action but are never the same as those actions, as a recent public letter by the English Anglican bishops makes clear, arguing in favor of policies that respect the natural environment, enhance human dignity, and honor the image of God in our neighbor, regardless of which political party proposes them.[6]

## PUBLIC SPHERE, PRIVATE SPHERE, AND RIGHTS

A discussion about religion and politics leads to further reflection about many different areas of life. Ramadan chooses to turn his attention next to the state of civil society. What he finds particularly striking is that at the same time as Muslim-majority societies are undergoing an identity crisis, the same is true of many Western societies, which are also facing an identity crisis as they face the presence of new religions and cultures, brought to them by the massive continued immigration that is necessary for them to survive. Topics such as pluralism, multiculturalism, and the common principles which undergird society are constantly resurfacing as political hot potatoes. He is clear there is a real danger in taking overly simplistic, poorly thought through stances, which are not robust enough to match up

---

4. Ibid., 265.
5. Williams, *Faith in the Public Square*, 308.
6. Anglican Bishops, "Who is my Neighbour?" 3.

to the reality of the modern world, and argues we must recognize that no public sphere is religiously or culturally neutral, and every minority is influenced by the common, majority culture and religion of that society. Thus Ramadan suggests that French Muslims are influenced by Roman Catholicism in the same way that British Muslims are by Anglicanism. Our concern should not, he argues, be to debate (or enforce) the religious and cultural neutrality of the public sphere, but instead to work for equal rights, and therefore equal access to power. He is therefore concerned that when examples of the pluralism of Islamic civilization are given, there is a realistic assessment of the balance of power implied.

The two most common examples are medieval Andalusia (in what is now Spain) and the Ottoman Empire, under Süleyman the Magnificent (died 1566). Both are often cited as examples of Islamic tolerance and religious pluralism. Ramadan's question—and indeed mine—is whether people of every religion experienced equal rights and respect, or whether non-Muslims were merely tolerated by their political overlords. Those who have power should use it for the good of all. I have often heard Muslims speak of Andalusia as an ideal of religious pluralism, but the reality is that Muslims had a superior status to Christians and Jews within that society, so it is questionable how equal a society it really was, as *dhimmi* (protected but second-class) status was enforced during this time, and only gradually disappeared under the Ottoman empire.[7] There is always a danger of rose tinted glasses dominating any return to historical ideals.

Reading Ramadan's observation about power as an Anglican cleric, and therefore a power holder within the British cultural system, it strikes me that there are a number of necessary responses. The first is a realistic assessment and recognition of my own power. Anglican clergy know that, even in post-Christian contemporary British society, we still have far more power than the average individual. In particular, Anglican orders can be a means of gaining access to those with political and civic power. This fact must be recognized and responded to. The second necessary response flows from this recognition: that power must not be used exclusively for one's own benefit, but rather should be used to benefit other groups, even those with whom one has religious differences. Third, one's own power must be used for the benefit of others. As with Rowan Williams' argument above, the Church is more credible as a witness to Christ when her power is used not for self, but willingly surrendered for the good of all.

7. Waardenburg, *Muslim Perceptions of Other Religions*, 18–76.

## What Kind of Friendship?

Ramadan returns to his fundamental reflection on the importance of respect for the dignity, welfare, freedom, equality, and justice for individuals.[8] These, he argues, should shape how civil society is organized. The dignity of people, their right to hold their own personal beliefs, and their right to self-expression and flourishing must all be guarded and protected. His concern is that if the public sphere aimed "to be so neutral as to forbid its members' free quest for coherence" then it would inevitably become oppressive and discriminatory. In a similar vein, Michael Nazir-Ali warns of the danger of promoting an empty tolerance that has isolated and ghettoized communities rather then facilitating integration and engagement.[9] Nick Spencer quotes Cardinal Cormac Murphy-O'Connor's 2007 Corbishley Lecture, where he voiced a similar concern: "My fear is that, under the guise of legislating for what is said to be tolerance, we are legislating for intolerance. Once this begins, it is hard to see where it ends. While decrying religion as dogmatic, is dogma to prevail in the public square, forcing to the margins the legitimate expression and practice of genuine religious conviction?"[10]

The risk is that enforced neutrality is in fact intolerant and therefore not really neutral, but an illiberal liberalism. Ramadan hopes that contemporary Muslim thinkers can lead the way in developing thinking about how to have a welcoming public space which is both politically pluralist and at the same time allows for religious diversity.

Nick Spencer's report *Neither Private nor Privileged* develops an argument that is remarkably similar to that developed by Ramadan. Spencer also rejects the twin delusions of complete separation and complete identification of religion and politics. He argues, on the basis of Acts 1–5, in favor of four strands of action: public proclamation, public assembly, public action, and public witness, noting also that public can, and sometimes does, also mean political involvement with the ruling powers. Spencer develops ideas of how contemporary Christianity might be present within contemporary political society. He does not argue for Christian control of political mechanisms, but for confident Christian involvement in policy making and political life, seeking to persuade of the value and legitimacy of Christian views, even if not everyone shares them.

---

8. Ramadan, *Radical Reform*, 270–1.
9. Nazir-Ali, *Triple Jeopardy*, 156.
10. Spencer, Neither Private Nor Privileged, 45.

Society, Education, and Power

## LAWS, POWER AND CIVIL SOCIETY

Ramadan is concerned that *shariah* has been reduced to simply "Islamic law," when he regards it more as "the Way to the light."[11] His concern is over the impact of legalism within the practice of Islam; devout Muslims should not, in his view, be concerned simply with theoretical box-ticking, but with wider issues of justice, peace, human dignity, freedom, and so forth. It is more important, he argues, that these higher objectives are reached, than that individuals engage in formalistic compliance to complex rules.

Ramadan outlines a debate that has been ongoing within Muslim-majority societies about the suitability of democracy as a model for political organization. There are a wide range of opinions, from those who reject it as overly Western, to those who see it as distorting the relationship with divinely given power, and those who want to develop a distinctively "Islamic democracy," ending with those who accept the Western model wholeheartedly. Ramadan himself is against either wholesale acceptance or rejection. He favors critical evaluation and development of an open and pluralistic political model, which includes some of Western democracy's strengths, while seeking to avoid its weaknesses.

It is interesting that Western Christians rarely criticize democracy as a system, despite the fact that this is not the only possible political system that is compatible with Christian belief. Perhaps we would benefit from listening carefully to the criticisms of those who are sufficiently removed from our own political activities that they can see the wood for the trees.

## THE ISLAMIC PENAL CODE (HUDUD) AND THE MORATORIUM

In March 2005, Tariq Ramadan launched a call for a moratorium on certain aspects of the Islamic Penal Code (*Hudud*), namely the death penalty, corporal punishment, and stoning in the Muslim world.[12] This was not warmly received by many Muslims, and he recalls in *Radical Reform* how much of the response to him engaged not with the substance of his argument, but criticized him either for suggesting a moratorium at all or for not going far enough (that is, for not calling for an outright ban).[13]

---

11. Ramadan, *Radical Reform*, 271–4.
12. Ramadan, "An International Call."
13. Ramadan, *Radical Reform*, 274–7.

The essence of Ramadan's argument in his call for a moratorium is that Islam is a message of equality and justice. His concern is that although the majority of religious teachers may claim that the restrictions around when the stipulations of *hudud* could actually be carried out mean it would almost never be applicable in real life; the reality is that many women and men are beaten, stoned, and executed in the name of *hudud*. That is to say, his concern that the misapplication of the Islamic penal code is being used to subvert the fundamental tenets of Islam concerning the dignity of people, and their right to equality and justice. He does not call for an outright ban, because he believes to do so would be to set himself up as having greater authority than the Qur'an, and he does not wish to do that. He recognizes the presence of texts within the Qur'an that do support the *hudud* (such as 24:2–3 which advocate one hundred lashes as punishment for adultery), and does not seek to abrogate or deny them. Rather, his concern is that until the proper conditions under which those texts apply can be clearly established by the majority of scholars, it is preferable to have a moratorium on the use of the punishments than to allow injustice to be perpetuated. The moratorium calls for work to be done, not for an unthinking change. The issues must be debated and evaluated, not left untouched.

Ramadan appears to have been hurt by some of the responses he received. He defends himself, arguing that he has not abandoned Islam, but has remained true to the methodology of decision making, asking the texts what they say, in what conditions can their stipulations be applied, and under what social context. What was possibly especially hurtful was the experience of scholars who supported his views in private, but then would not do so in public. His attempt at reform within Islam on the particularly difficult and fraught topic of capital punishment appears to have stumbled and stalled.

It would be easy, and foolish, for Christians reading of these debates to engage in any form of polemic or condemnation of the different sides. Christian history is full of examples of practices that are now regarded as abhorrent, being justified on the basis of appeal to sacred texts. Prime examples might be the practice of slavery and the segregation of apartheid. In both cases, the drive for change came when convinced believers returned to the sacred texts and read them more thoroughly and critically, asking precisely the questions Ramadan poses. It is true that slavery is mentioned in the Bible, but in what context and under what conditions was slavery permitted? Does the Bible encourage or condemn it, and how can that teaching be applied to our contemporary situation? I have so far deliberately used examples of debates that have now passed, but there are still many questions that Christians debate today, including the applicability of the death penalty, the right to physician-assisted suicide, issues of human sexuality, or whether particular wars can indeed be justified. What I take from Ramadan's call is an example of courage in challenging the status quo, and a willingness to be controversial. It is, to paraphrase Rowan Williams' argument about the Church above, arguably a good example of being credible but not popular in expressing Islamic faith. That does not mean simply conforming to the demands of wider society but always being willing to return to sacred texts to ensure one's views are based in Scripture, not personal prejudice.

## EDUCATION

Ramadan rightly argues that education is a fundamental building block of the reform he advocates.[14] Societies throughout the world, whether Muslims are in the majority or are a minority, have to accept diversity and debate their differences. The only way for this to be achieved is for everyone to have a voice and for people to be equipped to understand and engage with difference. Ramadan is scathing of the educational systems of many Muslim-majority societies, where there are both "unacceptable illiteracy rates" and "systems and methods that kill critical thinking and reinforce rote learning and social injustices."[15] What is needed is mass education, which enables both functional literacy and critical thinking.

State education is necessary for this to be achieved. Private Islamic schools may well teach the religion well, with classes on Qur'an, *ahadith*, the lives of the Prophets, morals, and so forth, but their pedagogy is that of the Western social and economic system based on selection and performance. Ramadan questions whether these schools can therefore be genuinely regarded as fully Islamic, since they primarily target and perpetuate the existence of a privileged elite without touching the masses who lack even the most basic education. Ramadan advocates educational institutions that are concerned with personal development, developing critical thinking, creativity, solidarity, and knowledge of and respect for others. His

---

14. Ibid., 278–80.
15. Ibid., 278.

concern is that the shallowness of much of the Western educational system is criticized, but then unthinkingly imitated by those selfsame critics.

There is a need, he argues, for Islamic schools that are founded upon genuinely Islamic principles. He summarizes his point as follows:

> A society that is intellectually, culturally, and politically open, that experiences true qualitative and human *development*, needs a school system and schools that promote such values and ethical principles and above all that do not end up yielding to the dictates of economy by being privatized or becoming obsessed with the specific, standardized production of "gray matter" just as some firms focus on producing raw materials. Respect for *diversity*, human *solidarity*, and cultural and artistic *creativity* should also be taught; such are the schools we need today, and they should combine traditional methods with more innovative approaches in order to take up the challenges of contemporary times.[16]

Ramadan's is not the only voice calling for a more genuine Islamic education. There are a number of other advocates of a genuinely Islamic pedagogy, of whom Maurice Irfan Coles is a representative example. A few years ago Coles produced a report entitled *Every Muslim Child Matters*, detailing how state school teaching could be more authentic to Islamic ideals. Christians are also increasingly voicing concern that much Western pedagogy is too mechanistic and that the worldview that lies behind it does not sit well with Christian principles. There is work on welcoming children of other faiths into Christian schools.[17] Within the United Kingdom, there is a program called *What if. . .? Learning*,[18] which seeks to shape the curriculum along genuinely Christian lines. The Kuyers Institute for Christian Teaching and Learning in the US also advocates similar work.

Trevor Cooling, head of the Christian Education unit in Canterbury Christ Church University, has also written on the topic. One of his more widely disseminated works is a report entitled *Doing God in Education*. In this report, Cooling outlines a number of examples of how a genuinely Christian worldview may change curriculum delivery. One concerns teaching of foreign languages. Rather than ask students to describe in German how they would spend a million euros, they were asked to describe how they would give it away. Similarly, a mathematics lesson on drawing pie

---

16. Ibid., 280.
17. Wilson, *All United Together*, sets out one such vision.
18. http://www.whatiflearning.co.uk/.

charts used the daily activities of an African mother and an English mother to help encourage empathy amongst students. Many more examples could be given, but the point is that all education is on the basis of a particular worldview, and even basic decisions about what work to set will either perpetuate or challenge pupils' assumptions about how the world works. Many others have done similar work, and Smith and Smith detail some of their efforts.[19]

## DEMOCRACY AND MEDIA

In this section Ramadan rightly recognizes that it is important to move on from debates about the meaning and applicability of particular understandings of democracy.[20] What is important is to remain faithful to the fundamental principles (rule of law, equality before the law, universal suffrage, limited mandate, and separation of powers) and the higher outcomes he has already discussed (dignity, welfare, freedom, equality).

What Muslims need to do, he argues, is work out how these fundamental principles and higher outcomes can be realized within contemporary Islamic society. As noted above, education is the foundation on which to build a society that is intellectually well equipped and politically active. Citizens must be aware of their responsibilities and rights; they must be able to engage in critical speech and participate in elections. Fundamentally, conditions must be established in which power can be challenged.

Ramadan regards democracy as a "generic system encompassing a set of organizational and institutional models for universal, fundamental values and principles."[21] It is not a value but the product of attempts to realize the values of freedom, equality, justice, and dignity. The way in which those values are realized can—and should—be subject to critique, especially if the model fails to achieve its stated goals. He argues that the history of democracy is filled with examples of failures to promote peace, from the conflict with neighboring states, and discrimination against women and the poor that characterized Athenian democracy, to the tendency of the modern democratic US to engage in conflicts throughout the world while also discriminating against the poor and racial minorities within its own society. Idealist discourse about the virtues of democracy tends to obscure

---

19. Smith and Smith, *Teaching and Christian Practices*.
20. Ramadan, *Radical Reform*, 280–5.
21. Ibid., 282.

the very real problems that exist within it, of which disengagement from and disenchantment with political processes is perhaps the most pressing.

Ramadan is clear that democracy is easily subverted to justify totalitarian ends. He recognizes that terrorism is a real evil that must be fought against, but suggests that at the same time it can be used to justify the most anti-democratic policies. He does not cite particular actions of the security services, but rather refers to the climate of fear and distrust that can be fostered by counter-terrorist work. Allen supports this, with a detailed discussion of the rise of Islamophobia in the UK.[22]

The power of the media is a particular concern of Ramadan's. While there is a wide range of news outlets, he argues that the reality is that they are owned by a restricted and secretive elite, whose actions in the world of economy and politics are rarely reported. Ramadan notes that while there may be no censorship as practiced by dictatorships, there is the control of editorial policies and protection of interests. Moreover, the tyranny of speed, the need to get a breaking news story out before anyone else does, means that opportunities for calm reflection and careful, nuanced analysis are rarely taken. Ramadan urges Muslim thinkers to engage in comprehensive thought about these complex issues. He is wary of solutions that simply repeat ideal Islamic values without engaging with the substance of the problems. Real reform, he believes, is both necessary and possible, but neither easy nor simple.

In a recent speech, the Archbishop of Canterbury, Justin Welby, observed that:

> A 21st-century global Church, with all Christians irrevocably belonging to each other through the action of God, seeking to discern truth in many thousand cultures, is a church with fuzzy edges; because in a world in which cultures overlap constantly, and are communicated instantly—and, judging from what I get, often with some friction—you need space to adapt and to meet with one another, and you have to trust the sovereign grace of God for the consequences. Comments that even twenty years ago took months to reach the far corners of the earth now, as we know, take seconds. Instant reaction has replaced reflective comment. That is a reality that you deal with in politics, and it demands a new reality of ways in which we accept one another, love each other, pray for each other. The best answer to a complex issue on which one has heard

---

22. Allen, *Islamophobia*.

## Society, Education, and Power

a soundbite from a sophisticated argument is not always given in 140 characters.[23]

Media power is a real force, which must be recognized and responded to. I can remember organizing a seminar for Christian and Muslim community activists, which stressed the positive opportunities that are available from engaging well with the media. The reality is that in the UK media, religious issues are likely to be dealt with by non-specialists, and faith issues, especially those relating to Islam, are invariably portrayed negatively.[24] Some may argue this reflects the fact that religious issues are now simply part of public life and do not need their own specialist, and it is certainly true that the national press tends only to report religious affairs as related to other news concerns (the economy, crime, discrimination against particular groups, and so forth). But at the same time, it is striking that many within the media do not think a specialist is required.

The fast-moving world of 24-hour-a-day news, coupled with the growth of both blogging and Twitter, make for a very complex world of interlocking power structures. Christians, together with Muslims, have much to reflect on and learn from each other about how best to promote faith in a climate that is not entirely conducive to doing so.

### POWERS AND COUNTERPOWERS

Ramadan believes the world has changed: globalization has transformed the nature and weight of different powers and how they interact with different human communities.[25] The problem, as he sees it, is that many Muslims have not yet realized the scale of these changes, and so when they discuss the dynamics of power distribution they remain wedded to older models. He suggests many Islamic reform movements, such as *Hizb at-Tahrir* or *al-Muhajirun*, operate on binary categories of Islamic and non-Islamic societies. Other Islamist movements, such as the Muslim Brotherhood in Egypt or Justice and Development in Turkey, still operate on a relationship to texts and political power that is based on early or mid-twentieth century models and modes of thinking.

---

23. Welby, "Archbishop's Address to the Parliamentary Prayer Breakfast."
24. Knott et al., *Media Portrayals*.
25. Ramadan, *Radical Reform*, 285–92.

Organizations founded on an immediately post-colonial, early independence agenda need to adapt and change, he argues, to the very different political climate of the early twenty-first century. The power of multinational corporations, of the media, of financial organizations, are often greater than those of nation states. The failure to recognize these realities means the problems cannot be dealt with. At the grassroots level, he notes, people no longer believe in the political discourse; they are increasingly disenchanted with the activities of a political elite and their love for power. The old ideologies may be passing away, but what is left is not a vacuum, but a shift in how political action takes place.

## WHAT KIND OF FRIENDSHIP?

Ramadan wants Muslims to be actively involved in this shift towards a new politics, in seeking creative solutions, in returning to their sacred texts for guidance, and principles that can be applied to the contemporary situation and its problems. We must be clear about the realities of what we face. "We must look squarely at humans, hypocrisies, and lies; we must simplify nothing."[26] There is no space for wide-eyed idealism, he argues, only pragmatic action to transform the world. Christians will agree with this. In the run up to the 2015 General Election in the UK, Andy Flannagan, a Christian actively involved in politics in the UK, published *Those Who Show Up*, which argues that only those who choose to actively involve themselves in politics have any chance of making a real difference. Although Flannagan himself is left wing in his politics, his book includes contributions from across the political spectrum, which I found to be a real strength. I am good friends with Christians who hold a wide variety of political views, and for Christianity to flourish, we need faithful disciples of all political persuasions to become active and engaged campaigners. Ramadan's challenge, to return to the Bible and discern guidance to bring about growth in the Kingdom of God on earth, is one I take seriously and would motivate my friendship with politically engaged Muslim friends.

---

26. Ibid., 292.

# 10

# Ethics and Universals

The reform presented in the course of this book must begin with reconciliation within the texts, their meaning, and their highest goals considered in history and in various human societies.[1]

RAMADAN SUGGESTS THAT MUSLIMS must struggle in particular against the restrictive imitation of past scholars, and against literalist reduction of their faith.[2] He does also recognize the source of these problems, which he identifies as fear of the sacred texts of Islam not being respected, concern about excessive influence of the West, or of a homogenized global culture. These are all concerns Ramadan himself also shares. He notes the problem of a confusion of religion and culture, of the myth of a single objective truthful reading of a text, and of interpretations that are so rarified they are of no practical application. These are all issues he has addressed in the course of his discussion of the need for *Radical Reform*.

Ramadan's fundamental premise is that Allah has created diversity and that this means it should be embraced and engaged with, not feared or excluded. He quotes the Qur'anic recognition of the diversity of nations and tribes (49:13), and suggests the resultant plurality of religions, skin colors, cultures, and languages all mean that "universality, which according to Muslims emanates from the last revealed religion, is necessarily open,

1. Ramadan, *Radical Reform*, 293.
2. Ibid., 293–313.

shared, inclusive, and dynamic, rather than fearful, exclusive, rigid and closed."[3]

Ramadan is not a Universalist, nor is he advocating a search for universal truths or values beyond individual religions. Rather he wishes to establish correspondences, intersections, and bridges. Reading this as a convinced Christian, I am reassured by his refusal to abandon his own core beliefs, because I believe that also gives me permission to hold onto mine. My experience of engaging with those of other faiths is that it is only after we acknowledge the nature of our personal (and very different) faith convictions that we can then begin to work on establishing the correspondences, intersections, and bridges between our beliefs. Honest recognition of difference is more empowering than disingenuous platitudes about similarity.

Ramadan describes the twofold movement of "determined self-assertion allied to confident opening up to all civilizations and religions,"[4] which I concur as an accurate description of the process. Islam and Christianity are both proselytizing religions, and it would be foolish to ignore this reality as we engage with each other. The guidelines for ethical witness, which I mentioned in the previous chapter, are designed to allow for confident religious exchange that is aiming both to learn from and to challenge the beliefs of the other. To engage in such debates is a risky and testing process, but the results are far more rewarding and enriching than sterile conversations that do not move beyond lowest common denominator similarity.

Islam is a textual religion, founded on belief of the revelation of a sacred text in a particular language to a particular individual. Ramadan expects everything a Muslim does and says should flow from interpretation of and engagement with this sacred text. This makes Islam a religion of intelligence and of reason, of serious intellectual work as well as of the heart.

Although both heart and head are involved in comprehending Islam, Ramadan suggests that the heart is primary. He states that the first reason that it receives the Revelation is not analytical reason but the reason of the heart, quoting the Qur'anic condemnation of those who do not receive the truth:

> Certainly We have created for Gehenna many of the jinn and humans: they have hearts, but they do not understand with them;

3. Ibid., 294.
4. Ibid., 295.

they have eyes, but they do not see with them; they have ears, but they do not hear with them. Those (people) are like cattle—No! They are (even) further astray! Those—they are the oblivious. (7:179)

His point is that faith is not solely about analytical or intellectual reason, it is about a changed heart. Once the heart is transformed, then how one reads the Qur'an, and also how one engages with the created world (Ramadan's second "book") changes completely. Ramadan seems to long particularly for Muslims to experience a transformation of the heart that would enable them to engage positively with those outside of their own faith. He recognizes, and repeatedly affirms, the validity of concerns about the neglect of sacred texts and about the marginalization of Muslims, but at the same time, he wants his fellow Muslims to have the courage to move beyond the comfort and security of only associating with their peers.

For Ramadan, the problem stems from a confusion of orders. He acknowledges, and affirms, that Qur'an's self-description as a complete revelation, but at the same time argues that this does not mean it reveals everything. Thus the Qur'an states: "We have sent down on you the Book as an explanation for everything, and as a guidance and mercy, and as good news for those who submit" (16:89).

But this, and other similar statements (such as 6:38) do not mean the Qur'an is a complete revelation of all scientific knowledge, Ramadan argues. Rather it indicates that the Qur'an provides guidance for any and every walk of life, orientating the conscience and illuminating the goals of science, without detailing the content of particular research.

In a similar vein, Ramadan argues that Islam has nothing to fear from philosophy, provided it is not an arid atheistic exercise, but one suffused with and engaged with the Revelation of the Qur'an. Thus the *shariah*, the Way of Islamic life, should not be reduced to a set of laws, but remain a Way of life rooted in the two Books of the Qur'an and the Universe, focusing and directing the conscience along the correct path.

A call to dialogue lies at the heart of *Radical Reform*: first, intra-religious dialogue, and second, inter-religious dialogue. Ramadan wants the different schools of thought within Islam to engage more constructively and productively with each other. He calls for a return to the fundamentals of the faith, to a focus on how the Prophet's Companions related to him, to the Qur'an, and to each other as a community of faith.

## What Kind of Friendship?

My experience of engaging with Muslims is that when one first encounters them, they will often talk about the unity that exists within Islam, and it is only on establishing a much stronger bond of trust that they start to be prepared to acknowledge and discuss the many differences that lie between them.[5] Ramadan is not advocating this kind of false, superficial unity. He suggests Muslims find it difficult to tolerate division, and urges them to open themselves up to a critical dialogue that accepts the diversity of views that exist among them. He urges Muslims to not simply unite in opposition to a perceived enemy (citing the controversy over the Danish cartoons of the Prophet as one example) but much more to unite together in working as positive forces for good. Without such positive intra-Muslim relations, the possibility of positive inter-faith relations is greatly reduced.

The call for intra- and inter-faith dialogue is not one that Ramadan makes exclusively to a Muslim audience. He expects Christians and those of other faiths or no faith to also engage in this process. He correctly notes that Western Europe is suffering from an identity crisis, a selective memory of the contribution of Muslims (and others) to the growth of civilization on the continent,[6] and real insecurity about both the present and the future. In essence, Ramadan's argument is that if Europe does not recognize the diversity of its history, we will struggle to reconcile the diversity of our present. This point is a valuable one, but constructing history is a difficult exercise. Albert Schweitzer is famed within historical Jesus studies for his observation that there has been a tendency amongst academics to reconstruct Jesus in their own image, and the same charge could be leveled at any historical project that is not careful to elucidate and engage with its own presuppositions. It is always tempting to build an account of the past in order to shape the present to our own preferences, and while there is truth in Ramadan's observation, we must be careful to ensure we ask the hard questions of both ourselves and others as we try and build and understanding of how our ancestors related in order to relate to one another in a more harmonious and understanding fashion.

Ramadan himself is not naïve. He does recognize the need for this sort of process, arguing for scientific rigor, thorough self-criticism, and concern to be coherent both in identifying problems and also concrete responses.

---

5. Ruthven, *Islam*, 78, states there are now five schools of jurisprudence within Islam: four Sunni (Shafi'i, Hanafi, Maliki and Hanbali) and one Shi'a (Ja'fari).

6. Lyons, *The House of Wisdom*.

## ETHICS AND UNIVERSALS

Radical reform is not a simple exercise, but a complex, cooperative, and challenging process.

### WHAT KIND OF FRIENDSHIP?

I have found reading Ramadan to be a complex and challenging process. His perspective is both very different from and also quite similar to my own. He, like me, is a person of convinced faith, but his faith is very different from mine. Some of our differences are superficial, and the fundamentals that are beneath them are similar. To cite an example from this book: I am not concerned whether the meat I eat has been slaughtered according to ritual practices, but I am concerned for animal welfare (which Ramadan argues undergirds the prescriptions around *halal* slaughter). I recognize the difficulty in engaging with the twin horizons of the text and contemporary context; although Christians do not argue about capital punishment as vehemently as Muslims might, they are engaged in controversy about human sexuality, and understandings of sacred texts lie at the heart of these discussions.

Some of Ramadan's writing is immensely challenging. Taking just one example, his call for a different economic model is one that many Christians (including myself) share. But the process of realizing that new model is a difficult one, which requires great intellectual effort and practical challenge. The issues are not simple, and the solution may be a long time in coming. My personal friendships with Muslims challenges my spiritual practices, not least the need for regular prayer and fasting. This may be a start, but there is much more to be done.

In his conclusion to *Radical Reform*, Ramadan calls for consciences to be awakened, to become open to question and assess the reality of our contemporary situation, and "ultimately to free ourselves from the mirages of time and the pressure of fashion."[7] Christians need to do this just as much as Muslims. Similarly, we all need to resist both evolution and progress devoid of conscience or soul on the one hand, and also rigid imitation and misleading formalist religion on the other. New is not necessarily better, but neither is unthinking adherence to old forms, devoid of the meaning with which they were once imbibed.

Reading Ramadan is a challenge to the Christian. He argues that faith should be allied with intelligence, enabling confident resistance of the twin

---

7. Ramadan, *Radical Reform*, 317.

dangers outlined above. He calls for energetic intellectual work, leading to true freedom, which "refuses alienation and mobilizes knowledge, human creativity, and ethical sense to transform the world and make it a better place."[8] The faith on which I base my desire to do this is different from Ramadan's. My vision of God's kingdom differs from Ramadan's. But there is still much that we have in common, and much we can work together to realize.

---

8. Ibid., 317.

# Bibliography

Abdul-Matin, Ibrahim. *Green Deen: What Islam Teaches about Protecting the Planet.* Markfield: Kube, 2012.
Al-Qaradawi, Yusuf. *The Lawful and the Prohibited in Islam.* Translated by Kamal El-Helbawy, M. Moinuddin Siddiqui and Syed Shukry. Reviewed by Ahmad Zaki Hammad. Kitab Bhavab: New Delhi, 2011.
Allen, Chris. *Islamophobia.* Farnham: Ashgate, 2010.
Anglican Bishops. "Who is my Neighbour?" A Letter from the House of Bishops to the People and Parishes of the Church of England for the General Election 2015. London: The Church of England, 2015. https://www.churchofengland.org/media/2170230/whoismyneighbour-pages.pdf.
Ansari, Humayun. *The Infidel Within: Muslims in Britain since 1800.* London: Hurst, 2004.
Badham, Paul. *Is there a Christian Case for Assisted Dying?* London: SPCK, 2009.
Bailey, Kenneth E,. *Poet and Peasant* and *Through Peasant Eyes: A Literary-Cultural Approach to the Parables in Luke.* Grand Rapids: Eerdmans, 1983.
———. *The Good Shepherd: A Thousand-Year Journey from Psalm 23 to the New Testament.* London: SPCK, 2015.
Baker, David L. *Tight Fists or Open Hands? Wealth and Poverty in Old Testament Law.* Grand Rapids: Eerdmans, 2009.
Behrend, Heike. *Alice Lakwena and the Holy Spirits: War in Northern Uganda 1986–97.* Oxford: James Currey, 1999.
Bellos, David. *Is That a Fish in Your Ear?* London: Penguin, 2009.
Biggar, Nigel. *Aiming to Kill: The Ethics of Suicide and Euthanasia.* London: DLT, 2004.
Bowen, Innes. *Medina in Birmingham, Najaf in Brent: Inside British Islam.* London: Hurst, 2014.
Bretherton, Luke. *Hospitality as Holiness: Christian Witness Amid Moral Diversity.* Farnham: Ashgate, 2010.
Bulman, Kate Harper and Christine McCourt. "Somali Refugee Women's Experiences of Maternity Care in West London: A Case Study" *Critical Public Health* 12 (2002) 365–80.
Cameron, Joan and Karen Rawlings Anderson. "'Circumcision,' Culture, and Health-Care Provision in Tower Hamlets, London," *Gender and Development* 6 (1998) 48–54.
Cesari, Jocelyne. *Why the West Fears Islam: An Exploration of Muslims in Liberal Democracies.* London: Palgrave Macmillan, 2013.

Chaplin, Jonathan. *Multiculturalism: A Christian Retrieval.* London: Theos, 2011.

———. *Talking God: The Legitimacy of Christian Public Reasoning.* London: Theos, 2009.

Coles, Maurice Irfan. *Every Muslim Child Matters: Practical Guidance for Schools and Children's Services.* Stoke on Trent: Trentham, 2008.

Common Worship. *Times and Seasons.* London: Church House Publishing, 2006.

Connor, Steve. *The Lost Girls: Illegal Abortion Widely Used by Some UK Ethnic Groups to Avoid Daughters 'Has Reduced Female Population by Between 1,500 and 4,700.'* The Independent Newspaper, Wednesday 15th January 2014. http://www.independent.co.uk/news/science/the-lost-girls-illegal-abortion-widely-used-by-some-uk-ethnic-groups-to-avoid-daughters-has-reduced-female-population-by-between-1500-and-4700–9059790.html.

Cooling, Trevor. *Doing God in Education.* London: Theos, 2010.

Crane, Robert Dickson. "From Clashing Civilisations to a Common Vision." In *Islam and Global Dialogue: Religious Pluralism and the Pursuit of Peace*, edited by Roger Boase, 159–77. Farnham: Ashgate, 2010.

D'Costa, Gavin. *Christianity and World Religions: Disputed Questions in the Theology of Religions.* Chichester: Wiley-Blackwell, 2009.

Drodge, A. J. *The Qur'an: A New Annotated Translation.* Sheffield: Equinox, 2013.

Flannagan, Andy. *Those Who Show Up.* Edinburgh: Muddy Pearl, 2015.

France, R. T. *New International Commentary on the New Testament: The Gospel of Matthew.* Grand Rapids: Eerdmans, 2007.

Fraser, Giles. *If Christianity is a Romance, Helping Those We Love to Die is an Abandonment.* The Guardian Newspaper. Friday 18th July 2014. http://www.theguardian.com/commentisfree/belief/2014/jul/18/christianity-romance-helping-love-die-abandonment.

Gadamer, Hans-Georg. *Truth and Method,* London: Continuum, 2004.

Geaves, Ron. *Aspects of Islam.* London: DLT, 2005.

———. *Islam in Victorian Britain: The Life and Times of Abdullah Quilliam.* Markfield: Kube 2010.

———. *Islam Today.* London: Continuum, 2010.

Gest, Justin. *Apart: Alienated and Engaged Muslims in the West.* London: Hurst, 2010.

Gilliat-Ray, Sophie. *Muslims in Britain: An Introduction.* Cambridge: Cambridge University Press, 2010.

Goddard, Lis and Clare Hendry. *The Gender Agenda: Discovering God's Plan for Church Leadership.* Nottingham: Intervarsity, 2010.

Greggs, Tom. "The Lord of All: Rediscovering the Christian Doctrine of Providence for the World." In *Transforming Exclusion: Engaging Faith Perspectives,* edited by Hannah Bacon, et al., 44–62. London: T & T Clark, 2011.

Grossman, Edith. *Why Translation Matters.* New Haven: Yale University Press, 2010.

Hage, Ghassan. *White Nation: Fantasies of White Supremacy in a Multicultural Society.* New York: Routledge, 2000.

Harvey, Lincoln. *A Brief Theology of Sport.* London: SPCK, 2014.

Hauerwas, Stanley. *The Hauerwas Reader,* edited by John Berkman and Michael Cartwright. Durham: Duke University Press, 2001.

———. *Learning to Speak Christian.* London: SCM, 2011.

Hays, Richard B. *The Moral Vision of the New Testament: A Contemporary Introduction to New Testament Ethics.* London: T & T Clark, 1996.

# Bibliography

Jardim, Georgina L. *Recovering the Female Voice in Islamic Scripture: Women and Silence.* Farnham: Ashgate, 2014.

Jensen, Michael P. *Martyrdom and Identity: The Self on Trial.* London: T & T Clark, 2010.

Johnsdotter, Sara. "Somali Women in Western Exile: Reassessing Female Circumcision in the Light of Islamic Teachings." *Journal of Muslim Minority Affairs* 23 (2003) 361–73.

Knott, Kim, et al. *Media Portrayals of Religion and the Secular Sacred: Representation and Change.* Farnham: Ashgate, 2013.

Lamptey, Jerusha Tanner. *Never Wholly Other: A Muslima Theology of Religious Pluralism.* Oxford: Oxford University Press, 2014.

Lewis, Phil. *Young, British and Muslim.* London: T & T Clark, 2007.

Lyons, Jonathan. *The House of Wisdom: How the Arabs Transformed Western Civilization.* London: Bloomsbury, 2010.

Patrick, Anne E. *Conscience and Calling: Ethical Reflections on Catholic Women's Church Vocations.* London: T & T Clark, 2013.

Mahmood, Hamid. 2012. *The Dars-e Nizami and the Transnational, Traditionalist Madaris.* MA Diss., Queen Mary, University of London, 2012.

March, Andrew F. *Islam and Liberal Citizenship: The Search for an Overlapping Consensus.* Oxford: Oxford University Press, 2009.

Modood, Tariq. *Multiculturalism and Integration: Struggling with Confusions.* Bristol: Centre for the Study of Ethnicity and Citizenship, 2011.

Muller, Roland. *Honor and Shame: Unlocking the Door.* Xlibris, 2000.

Musk, Bill. *Touching the Soul of Islam.* London: Monarch, 2005.

Nazir-Ali, Michael. *Triple Jeopardy for the West: Aggressive Secularism, Radical Islamism and Multiculturalism.* London: Bloomsbury, 2012.

Newbigin, Lesslie. *The Gospel in a Pluralist Society.* London: SPCK, 1989.

Nida, Eugene. *Toward a Science of Translating: With Special Reference to Principles and Procedures Involved in Bible Translating.* Leiden: Brill, 1964.

Northcott, Michael S. *A Political Theology of Climate Change.* London: SPCK, 2014.

Osborne, Grant R. *The Hermeneutical Spiral: A Comprehensive Introduction to Biblical Interpretation.* Downers Grove: IVP Academic, 2006.

Pattison, Stephen. *Saving Face: Enfacement, Shame, Theology.* Farnham: Ashgate, 2013.

Peterson, Eugene. H. *Five Smooth Stones for Pastoral Work.* Grand Rapids: Eerdmans, 1980.

———. *Under the Unpredictable Plant: An Exploration in Vocational Holiness.* Grand Rapids: Eerdmans, 1992.

———. *Working the Angles: The Shape of Pastoral Integrity.* Grand Rapids: Eerdmans, 1987.

Rahner, Karl. *Theological Investigations 5.* London: DLT, 1966.

Ramadan, Tariq. *The Arab Awakening: Islam and the New Middle East.* London: Allen Lane, 2012.

———. *In the Footsteps of the Prophet: Lessons from the Life of Muhammad.* Oxford: Oxford University Press, 2007.

———. "An International Call for Moratorium on Corporal Punishment, Stoning and the Death Penalty in the Islamic World." http://tariqramadan.com/english/2005/04/05/an-international-call-for-moratorium-on-corporal-punishment-stoning-and-the-death-penalty-in-the-islamic-world/.

———. *Islam, the West and the Challenges of Modernity.* Leicester: The Islamic Foundation, 2001.

# Bibliography

———. *The Quest for Meaning: Developing a Philosophy of Pluralism*. London, Allen Lane, 2010.

———. *Radical Reform: Islamic Ethics and Liberation*. Oxford: Oxford University Press, 2009.

———. *To Be a European Muslim*. Leicester: The Islamic Foundation, 1999.

———. *Western Muslims and the Future of Islam*. Oxford: Oxford University Press, 2004.

———. *What I Believe*. Oxford: Oxford University Press, 2010.

Rawlings, Phil. *Engaging with Muslims: Building Cohesion while Seeking Conversion*. Cambridge: Grove, 2014.

Rosner, Bryan S. *Greed as Idolatry: The Origin and Meaning of a Pauline Metaphor*. Grand Rapids: Eerdmans, 2007.

Ruthven, Malise. *Islam: A Very Short Introduction*. Oxford: Oxford University Press, 1997.

Sahin, Abdullah. "Islam, Secularity and the Culture of Critical Openness: A Muslim Theological Reflection." In *British Secularism and Religion: Islam, Society and the State* edited by Yahya Birt, et al., 3–24. Markfield: Kube, 2011.

Saunders, Doug. *The Myth of the Muslim Tide: Do Immigrants Threaten the West?* New York: Vintage, 2012.

Sen, Amartya. *Identity and Violence: The Illusion of Destiny*. London: Penguin, 2006.

Smith, David I. and James K. A. Smith. *Teaching and Christian Practices: Reshaping Faith and Learning*. Grand Rapids: Eerdmans, 2011.

Spencer, Nick. *Neither Private nor Privileged: The Role of Christianity in Britain Today*. London: Theos, 2008.

Strange, Dan. *"For Their Rock is not as Our Rock": An Evangelical Theology of Religions*. Nottingham: Apollos, 2014.

Sullivan, John. "Catholic Education as Ongoing Translation." *International Studies in Catholic Education* 4 (2012) 200–7.

Tangney, June Price and Ronda L. Dearing. *Shame and Guilt*. New York: Guilford, 2002.

Tarlo, Emma. *Visibly Muslim: Fashion, Politics, Faith*. Oxford: Berg, 2010.

Thiessen, Elmer. *The Ethics of Evangelism: A Philosophical Defence of Ethical Proselytizing and Persuasion*. Milton Keynes: Paternoster, 2011.

Thiselton, Anthony C. *Hermeneutics*. Grand Rapids: Eerdmanns, 2009.

———. *New Horizons in Hermeneutics*. London: Harper Collins, 1992.

———. *The Two Horizons: New Testament Hermeneutics and Philosophical Description*. Carlisle: Paternoster, 1980.

Vanhoozer, Kevin J. *Is There a Meaning in This Text?* Grand Rapids: Zondervan, 1998.

Volf, Miroslav. *Allah: A Christian Response*. New York: Harper Collins, 2011.

Waardenburg, Jacques. *Muslim Perceptions of Other Religions: A Historical Survey*. Oxford: Oxford University Press, 1999.

Welby, Justin. "Archbishop's Address to the Parliamentary Prayer Breakfast." http://www.archbishopofcanterbury.org/articles.php/5348/archbishops-address-to-parliamentary-prayer-breakfast.

———. "The Good Economy." Speech delivered at Church House, Westminster, on Wednesday 4th February 2015. http://www.archbishopofcanterbury.org/articles.php/5487/ archbishop-of-canterburys-speech-on-the-good-economy.

Whang, Y. C. "To Whom is a Translator Responsible—Reader or Author?" In *Translating the Bible: Problems and Prospects* edited by Stanley E. Porter et al, 46–62. London: T & T Clark International, 1999.

# Bibliography

Williams, Jenni. *God Remembered Rachel: Women's Stories in the Old Testament and Why They Matter.* London: SPCK, 2013.

Williams, Rowan. *Faith in the Public Square.* London: Bloomsbury, 2012.

———. "'Shariah law'—What did the Archbishop Actually Say?" http://rowanwilliams.archbishopofcanterbury.org/articles.php/1135/sharia-law-what-did-the-archbishop-actually-say.

Wilson, Tom. *All United Together: Christian Ministry in Multicultural Schools.* Gloucester: Wide Margin, 2013.

———. *Hospitality and Translation: An Exploration of How Muslim Pupils Translate their Faith in the Context of an Anglican Primary School.* Newcastle-Upon-Tyne, Cambridge Scholars, 2015.

Wright, N. T. "How Can the Bible be Authoritative?" *Vox Evangelica* 21 (1991) 7–32.

Yong, Amos. *Hospitality and the Other: Pentecost, Christian Practices, and the Neighbor.* New York: Orbis, 2008.

www.ingramcontent.com/pod-product-compliance
Lightning Source LLC
Chambersburg PA
CBHW071509150426
43191CB00009B/1454